Schriften des Jüdischen Museums Berlin

Band 2

Jüdisches Museum Berlin

»Höre die Wahrheit, wer sie auch spricht«

Stationen des Werks von Moses Maimonides vom islamischen Spanien bis ins moderne Berlin

Herausgegeben von Lukas Muehlethaler
im Auftrag des Jüdischen Museums Berlin

Vandenhoeck & Ruprecht

Mit 5 Abbildungen

Bibliografische Information der Deutschen Nationalbibliothek

Die Deutsche Nationalbibliothek verzeichnet diese Publikation in der Deutschen Nationalbibliografie; detaillierte bibliografische Daten sind im Internet über http://dnb.dnb.de abrufbar.

ISBN 978-3-525-30067-1

Weitere Ausgaben und Online-Angebote sind erhältlich unter: www.v-r.de

Gefördert durch die Beauftragte der Bundesregierung für Kultur und Medien.

Mit Unterstützung der Gesellschaft der Freunde und Förderer der Stiftung Jüdisches Museum Berlin e. V.

Umschlagabbildung: Die Akademie des Jüdischen Museums Berlin
Jüdisches Museum Berlin, Foto: Jens Ziehe

Satz: textformart, Göttingen | www.text-form-art.de
Druck und Bindung: CPI buchbücher.de, Birkach

Gedruckt auf alterungsbeständigem Papier.

Inhalt

Cilly Kugelmann

Grußwort

»Höre die Wahrheit, wer sie auch spricht.« Diese Worte sind in fünf Sprachen, groß und sichtbar an der Fassade der Akademie des Jüdischen Museums Berlin zu sehen. In modernem Hebräisch, im judeo-arabischen Original, das, wie alle jüdischen Sprachen, mit hebräischen Buchstaben geschrieben wird, in Arabisch, Englisch und Deutsch steht das Zitat für die Haltung, mit der neue Erkenntnisse und Forschung in die Arbeit des Museums integriert werden.

Das Zitat stammt von Mosche ben Maimon, der als Maimonides und mit seinem Kürzel »Rambam«, dem Akronym seines hebräischen Namens, in die Geschichte eingegangen ist.

1135 in Cordoba geboren und 1204 in Kairo gestorben, wurde er auf eigenen Wunsch in Tiberias begraben, wo heute noch sein Grab zu besichtigen ist. Maimonides war, wie alle großen Denker, deren Schriften noch nach vielen Jahrhunderten studiert werden, ein strittiger und umstrittener Mann. Als einer der wichtigsten mittelalterlichen jüdischen Philosophen verehrt, war er vielen auch verhasst, die ihn wegen seiner unorthodoxen Auslegung der jüdischen Gesetze als Abweichler und Ketzer betrachteten.

Neben seinem Brotberuf als Arzt, zu dessen Patienten auch der Sultan von Ägypten und sein Sekretär zählten, befasste er sich mit medizinischer Ethik, mit der Interpretation des Talmud, der Astronomie, der Philosophie und der Mathematik.

Sein bewegtes Leben, das durch mehrere Vertreibungen gekennzeichnet ist, öffnete ihm die Augen für eine humanistische und aufgeklärte Sicht auf die Probleme der Zeit und das tragische Schicksal seiner Glaubensgenossen.

Im Alter von 13 Jahren floh er das erste Mal mit seiner Familie vor einer radikal islamistischen Gesetzgebung, die den spanischen Christen und Juden die Ausübung ihrer Religion verbat und sie zwang, sich zum Islam zu bekennen. Das war auch das erste Mal, dass er sich mit einem Sendschreiben gegen einen Rabbiner nicht nur Freunde machte. Jener Rabbiner verurteilte den verzweifelten Scheinübertritt seiner Glaubensgenossen zum Islam als Götzendienst und verlangte von ihnen, dass sie den Märtyrertod einem Übertritt vorziehen müssten.

Maimonides dagegen zeigte tiefes Mitgefühl für diese Menschen, er verurteilte sie nicht, und zeigte im Gegenteil Verständnis dafür, dass sie mit allen Mitteln ihr Leben und das ihrer Familien retten wollten. Seiner Auffassung nach sollte die Einhaltung religiöser Gebote nicht zu Negativem dienen. »Der Mensch sollte mit den göttlichen Geboten leben, nicht sterben« schrieb er und empfahl in die Zukunft und nicht in die Vergangenheit zu schauen, wenn er sagte »Die Augen sind vorne, nicht hinten«.

Mit unserer neuen Schriftenreihe sind wir den philosophischen und kulturellen Aspekten der jüdischen Diaspora auf der Spur. Der zweite Band ist dem großen jüdischen Philosophen gewidmet, dessen Haltung einer kompromisslosen Offenheit der Wahrheit gegenüber wir als Leitmotiv für unsere Arbeit sehen: »Bei wissenschaftlichen Resultaten ist kein Unterschied, ob sie von Propheten oder nichtjüdischen Weisen, oder gar von Götzendienern stammen.«

Die Idee zu einem Zitat an der Wand der Akademie hatten der Architekt Daniel Libeskind und seine Frau Nina, die dem Museum nicht nur die bedingungslose Suche nach der Wahrheit mit auf den Weg gegeben haben. Sie haben diese Widmung dem Museum zum Geschenk gemacht, wofür wir Ihnen an dieser Stelle unseren Dank aussprechen.

Lukas Muehlethaler

Introduction

This slender volume introduces you to unfamiliar aspects of Moses Maimonides and of Jewish and non-Jewish readers of his work—especially if you know Maimonides only by name or have never heard of him at all.

Moses Maimonides, who was born in Muslim Spain and died in the year 1204 in Old Cairo, is a towering figure in Jewish culture. His person and his contributions to law, exegesis, philosophy, and medicine reverberate beyond his time and place, from Muslim Spain to modern Berlin.

The title of the volume, "Hear the truth, whoever speaks it," borrows from an adjuration by Maimonides. It appears in his Arabic commentary on the Mishnaic tractate *Chapters of the Fathers*, a famous collection of ethical maxims by the early rabbinic sages. Maimonides declares that even though he will be quoting many different authorities—religious scholars and philosophers, Jews and non-Jews—, he will refrain from marking these quotations. For the reader might reject the truth of a quotation simply out of his contempt for the person who first uttered it. Not only would this come as a disservice to the reader, it would also clash with Maimonides' ideal that one should "hear the truth, whoever speaks it."

Maimonides' adjuration was chosen as the title of this volume for two reasons. First, the adjuration is the reason why this slender volume came to be.

When the Jewish Museum Berlin was transforming the former flower market hall (*Blumengroßmarkthalle*) of Berlin into a building to house the museum's new Academy, the architect Daniel Libeskind approached me for a saying by Maimonides that would serve as a motto for the Academy as well as an inscription on the façade of the new building. I suggested—together with my colleague Gregor Schwarb, who is also contributing to this volume,—Maimonides' adjuration. If you approach the building of the Academy (or take a peek at the book cover) you will see to the left of the entrance the adjuration in the original Arabic—both in Arabic and Hebrew letters—as well as its Hebrew, English, and German translations in a design by Daniel Libeskind.

On 18 November 2012, the opening of the Academy was celebrated with a colloquium that explored Maimonides' adjuration as its motto. This event resulted from the collaboration between the Museum and the Research Unit Intellectual History of the Islamicate World at the Freie Universität Berlin. The collaboration extended to a second Maimonides colloquium held on 9 June

2013 to complement the scope of the first. The contributions collected in this book thus have their origin in presentations given at these two events.

The second and more significant reason prompting us to choose the adjuration by Maimonides as the title of the volume is that to "hear the truth, whoever speaks it" encapsulates the thematic focus of the contributions it collects.

While the first contribution provides merely some context on Maimonides' life and his adjuration, the second and third contributions consider Maimonides' adjuration in the light of his interaction with the majority culture in Muslim Spain and North Africa and ask what influence it had on his cultural outlook:

Maribel Fierro inquires into the "Almohadism" of Maimonides. The Almohads, a Berber dynasty from North Africa, emphasized the unity and incorporeality of God. They had started to wrestle control of Muslim Spain from their predecessors, the Almoravids, when Maimonides was still a boy. Because Maimonides continued to live in the Almohad sphere of influence into adulthood, Fierro reflects to what extent the cultural and religious policies of the Almohads had an influence on the outlook of Maimonides.

Sarah Stroumsa starts from one aspect of the Almohad religious policy, the forced conversions of Christians and Jews, to consider the cultural consequences of non-voluntary conversions. While living under Almohad rule, Maimonides and his family converted to Islam or at the very least had to hide their Jewish identity. Stroumsa suggests that Maimonides' own experience with conversion is reflected in his depiction of Abraham as the "patron of converts" away from polytheism. She also argues that non-voluntary conversions create new ways of intercultural exchange.

The adjuration to "hear the truth, whoever speaks it" captures not only Maimonides' own intellectual outlook, but also that of his readers. It is largely underappreciated that the readership of Maimonides' works, and especially of his famous *Guide of the Perplexed* (*Dalālat al-ḥā'irīn, Moreh Nevukhim*), was not restricted to Jews. The following three contributions therefore look at non-Jewish readers of Maimonides, in particular Muslims, Arab Christians, as well as Latin schoolmen.

Gregor Schwarb summarizes the results of his research on the reception of Maimonides among the representatives of the 13th-century Coptic renaissance. He shows that the Coptic priest, physician, and secretary Abū l-Ḫayr Ibn al-Ṭayyib quotes from Maimonides' *Guide of the Perplexed* and appropriates Maimonides' take on the principle of accommodation, which holds that divine revelation adjusts to the historical and social circumstances of its addressees.

My own text points out that Muslim authors writing in Arabic were among the earliest readers of the *Guide*. It focuses on the 13th-century Muslim physician, astronomer, and philosopher Muḥammad b. Abī Bakr al-Tabrīzī who commented extensively on 25 philosophical premises that open the second part of Maimonides' *Guide of the Perplexed.* I show that al-Tabrīzī interprets Maimonides' premises with the methods and within the doctrinal framework of 13th-century Avicennan philosophy.

Görge Hasselhoff looks at the reception of Maimonides' *Guide of the Perplexed* in the West, where the work became available in Latin translation in the generation after Maimonides. Hasselhoff traces the Latin translations of the *Guide* and other works of Maimonides, as well as their readers, down to the 15th century. This allows him to distinguish three distinct periods in the Christian reception of Maimonides, each espousing its own image of Maimonides on the basis of a selection of texts.

The final two contributions look at the re-discovery of Maimonides' *Guide of the Perplexed* among 18th and 19th-century Jews in Germany with particular reference to Berlin.

Yitzhak Y. Melamed considers two readers of Maimonides' works: Benedict de Spinoza in the 17th century and Salomon Maimon in the 18th century. Melamed presents them as heirs to a radical interpretation of Maimonides that sees as his main concern the unfettered pursuit of truth. In the case of Salomon Maimon, this Maimonidean radicalism was encouraged by his acquaintance with Spinoza's philosophy. This led him to clash with the representatives of the Jewish Enlightenment in Berlin and to his departure from the city.

George Y. Kohler closes the volume with a contribution on the German-Jewish rediscovery of Maimonides' religious philosophy since the middle of the 18th century. He shows that Maimonides was central to the liberal and rational interpretation of Judaism by the Jewish Neo-Kantian philosopher Hermann Cohen who died in the year 1918 in Berlin. Kohler argues that in Cohen's *Religion of Reason out of the Sources of Judaism* the German-Jewish rediscovery of Maimonides reaches its climax.

While these contributions present often unknown or underappreciated aspects of Maimonides and incorporate original and at times recent research they are directed at a general readership. The interested reader can follow the references at the beginning of each contribution to the glossary entries. The glossary was written by Filip Kaźmierczak and Hanna Zoe Trauer with the general reader in mind. The glossary provides some helpful context and reference to further readings, but it does not intend to be an exhaustive or up-to-date reference work on the terms defined.

The volume contains contributions in both English and German. For editorial reasons it was decided to publish the contributions in the language in which they were originally written and presented. The abstracts as well as the glossary try to make the contributions accessible also to speakers of the other language. Some contributions give Arabic and Hebrew names and terms in transcription. In general, German transcriptions follow the rules of the *Deutsche Morgenländische Gesellschaft* and English transcriptions those of the *Library of Congress*. However, authors were asked to follow the system they are most familiar with and no attempt was made to unify usage across contributions.

It remains what is certainly the most pleasant task of an editor: to thank all those who have made the publication of this volume possible. My gratitude goes to Daniel Libeskind for asking the question that ultimately led to this volume and for speaking at the Maimonides Colloquium; to Lev Libeskind for his initiative and enthusiasm which brought and kept everything in motion; to Cilly Kugelmann and Signe Rossbach of the Jewish Museum Berlin for their unconditional support of the colloquia and the volume alike; to Sabine Schmidtke of the Research Unit Intellectual History of the Islamicate World for her dedication to the approach this volume reflects; to Filip Kaźmierczak and Hanna Zoe Trauer, my collaborators at the "Arbeitsbereich" Jewish philosophy and aesthetics, for writing the glossary and contributing in many other ways; to the participants of both Maimonides Colloquia, which also included Sari Nusseibeh and Claudia Roden, for coming to Berlin and sharing the passion for their research with a broader audience; and to Peter Adamson for moderating the first Colloquium with incomparable gusto.

I am especially indebted to Maribel Fierro, Görge Hasselhoff, George Kohler, Yitzhak Melamed, Gregor Schwarb, and Sarah Stroumsa for their time and devotion to gearing their contributions toward a general readership, and first and foremost to Christine Marth and Marie Naumann of the Jewish Museum Berlin for their effort, patience and encouragement while seeing the volume to press.

The Maimonides Colloquia, as well as the work on this volume, was supported by funds from the Jewish Museum Berlin, the European Research Council's FP7 grant "Rediscovering Theological Rationalism in the World of Islam," the Bundesministerium für Bildung und Forschung, the Center for International Cooperation at the Freie Universität Berlin, and the Zentrum Jüdische Studien Berlin-Brandenburg. Their support is gratefully acknowledged here.

Lukas Muehlethaler

"Hear the Truth, Whoever Speaks It" On Moses Maimonides and his Adjuration

► Almohads ► Almoravids ► Berbers ► al-Fārābī ► Genizah ► Midrash ► Mishnah ► Rabbinic ► Talmud

Maimonides is one of the best-documented Jewish figures from the Middle Ages. Because of his eminent standing, none of his published works were lost and some are even extant as autographs. Moreover, there are reports about Maimonides from contemporaries both inside and outside of the Jewish community. And finally, luck as well as the climate of Egypt, preserved in the Cairo Genizah personal letters in his own handwriting, originals of his legal opinions, and passages from his major works as early drafts. Yet this relative wealth of information poses its own problems. The reports about the circumstances of Maimonides' life are often conflicting and at times outright contradictory.

And as it goes with any towering figure: Many step up to claim them for their own cause. As a result, throughout the centuries we find a great number of different perceptions and images of Maimonides. All have some basis in what we consider historic reality. But they differ from each other — sometimes to such an extent that we find it difficult to relate them to a single person who actually existed. There is — as it is sometimes quipped with a remark attributed to Shlomo Rosenthal — not only "My-monides," there is also "Your-monides," "Her-monides," "Our-monides," and "Their-monides".

Which comes to say that these introductory remarks on Moses Maimonides and his adjuration "Hear the truth, whoever speaks it" provide only one perspective on Maimonides, namely "My-monides".[1] It is hoped that the contributions to this volume will further revise or shatter these images.

1 The reader is encouraged to explore further perspectives through the works listed in this and the following footnotes, from which I derived the information presented here: Carlos Fraenkel (ed.), Traditions of Maimonideanism, Leiden, Brill 2009; Moshe Halbertal, Maimonides: Life and Thought, Princeton, Princeton University Press 2014; Görge Hasselhoff (ed.), Moses Maimonides interkulturell gelesen (Interkulturelle Bibliothek, Bd. 20), Nordhausen, Bautz 2009; Joel L. Kraemer, Maimonides: The Life and World of One of Civilization's Greatest Minds, New York, Doubleday 2008; Sarah Stroumsa, Maimonides in His World: Portrait of a Mediterranean Thinker, Princeton, Princeton University Press 2009.

Maimonides' Life and Work

Moses Maimonides was born at some time between September 1136 and September 1137 in the city of Cordova in Muslim Spain. Since his father's name was Maymūn, he came to be known as Moses son of Maymūn or Mūsā ibn Maymūn. The corresponding Hebrew name is Moshe ben Maimon which, in rabbinic circles, is often rendered by the acrostic RAMBAM (Rabbi Moshe ben Maimon). In the Latin West, on the other hand, he has become known as Moses Maimonides, the form used in many Western languages.

At the time of Maimonides' birth much of Muslim Spain was under the rule of the Almoravids (Arabic: *Al-Murābiṭūn*). Originally a confederation of Berber tribes from North Africa, they had been called in the eleventh century by local Muslim rulers to halt the advance of Christian Castile from the North and subsequently decided to stay. But another Berber dynasty, the Almohads (Arabic: *al-Muwaḥḥidūn*), had already started to make themselves known. By 1160 they controlled large parts of North Africa and by 1173 most of Muslim Spain. The Almohad takeover of Muslim Spain that started in 1146 proved to be a time of hardship for the entire population and especially (as we will hear later today) for the non-Muslim population.

For the first thirty years of Maimonides' life, we have only the most general ideas of his whereabouts and activities. At some point during the Almohad conquest, Maimonides' family left Muslim Spain. We don't know their exact itinerary. But we know that the family spent some time in Fez around the year 1160 and we know that Maimonides, together with his father and brother David, paid a visit to the city of Jerusalem. Around the year 1164, the family settled in Egypt, in the city of Fusṭāṭ, today part of Old Cairo.

During that time, Maimonides had been studying medicine and, by observing his father and by his own diligent study, had become an authority of Jewish law. At the age of 23 he had commenced composing a commentary on the Mishnah. Maimonides worked on this commentary for seven years and completed it when he was 30 years of age.

He then returned to an idea he had been entertaining for some time: to write a comprehensive compilation of Jewish law. Perhaps as a preparatory work he first composed the *Book of Commandments*. In this work he identifies and explains the 613 commandments which, according to tradition, Moses had been given at Sinai.

Thus prepared Maimonides launched himself into the monumental task of writing his compilation. In scope it was to go far beyond the *Book of Commandments* and to present in a systematic way all precepts that guide or used to guide Jewish life, including those in the Mishnah, those in the Babylonian and the Palestinian Talmud, as well as those in rabbinic literature up to his own time. Maimonides worked ten years "day and night," as he states, to complete this work. And indeed it truly is a monumental achievement. It casts centuries of legal thought and practice into one systematic work written in lucid Hebrew prose.

Maimonides had no doubts about the importance of his work. He named it *Mishneh Torah* which can be translated as "Re-iteration of the Torah." The name reveals what Maimonides intended his composition to accomplish: to serve as the ultimate and generally understandable compilation of oral rabbinic law and to complement the first, written, Torah. All other compilations and codes would be rendered superfluous. "In the time to come," Maimonides writes in a letter to his favorite student, Joseph ben Judah, "all Israel will use only my composition, and every other will undoubtedly be disregarded."[2] It is interesting to note, that when it comes to scientific content, of which there is a great amount in the *Mishneh Torah*, Maimonides follows the principle he had already established in his Commentary on the Mishnah: "it makes no difference who the author is, whether prophets or gentiles framed the proofs. For when the reason for something is set forth clearly and its truth is known through faultless proof, we do not rely on the author, but on the proof."[3]

But because Maimonides also decided to omit all references to the rabbinic authorities whose views he presented in the *Mishneh Torah* his work attracted severe criticism. This reaction to the completed *Mishneh Torah* was a severe disappointment to Maimonides. But an event that occurred as he was putting the final touches to this work was proved much more devastating: his beloved brother David died in a shipwreck in the Indian Ocean.

The loss of his brother and its financial consequences must have forced Maimonides, now in his 40s, to look beyond scholarship. During that time it seems that Maimonides increased his medical practice for which he became well regarded even at court.

But despite having to earn a livelihood, caring for an extended family, and serving as a rabbinic judge (work for which he declined payment), Maimonides found time to write yet another major work: His *Guide for the Perplexed* (*Dalālat al-ḥa'irīn, Moreh Nevukhim*) which he wrote in Arabic — using Hebrew letters — and completed around 1191.

The *Guide* is often described as a book of philosophy, but its scope is much broader: it includes the philosophical explanation of difficult biblical words and passages as well as philosophical theology. Maimonides dedicated the work to his pupil Joseph ben Judah "and those like him" who had received both a religious education and some philosophical education and were left

2 Translation by Herbert A. Davidson, Moses Maimonides: The Man and His Works, New York, Oxford University Press 2005, 280.

3 Ibid, 227–228.

wondering, how the two could fit together. Maimonides is adamant they in fact do fit together. But ever since readers and scholars have been debating, how exactly Maimonides had thought they would join.

Be that as it may, the impact of this work was immense also in the West. It was translated into Hebrew by Samuel Ibn Tibbon in Southern France during the lifetime of Maimonides and was read, by proponents and opponents of Maimonides alike. There are few Jewish philosophers writing in Hebrew (or in Arabic, for that matter) who do not relate in some way to the *Guide*.

After completing the *Guide*, Maimonides' literary output decreased, and he came to focus mainly on medical works. His work as a physician both in private practice and at court, as well as the demands put upon him by his standing as the legal authority of his time occupied all of his time. We find him complaining in a letter to his favorite disciple, Joseph ben Judah, that he found very little time for the study of the Torah and the sciences. Not much changed during the last decade of his life, though illnesses increasingly began to affect him. He died In the year 1204 in Fusṭāṭ at the age of 66 or 67.

Maimonides had married the sister of his friend Abū Maʿālī who had in turn married Maimonides' sister. Unfortunately, we know nothing about Maimonides' wife other than the fact that she bore him a son, Abraham, who himself became a physician, a thinker, and an important figure in the Jewish community of Egypt. He started a line of prominent descendants of Maimonides that can be traced down to the 15th century.

Maimonides' Adjuration

As mentioned in the introduction to this volume, Maimonides wrote the adjuration "Hear the truth, whoever speaks it," in the introduction to his *Eight Chapters* (*Shemonah Perakim*), a short treatise on philosophical psychology and ethics. Even though the *Eight Chapters* are often read as an independent work, Maimonides conceived them as part of his Arabic commentary on the Mishnah. There the *Eight Chapters* precede his comments on the Mishnaic tractate *Chapters of the Fathers* (*Pirkei Avot*), a widely-read collection of ethical maxims by early rabbinic authorities.

At first sight, Maimonides' adjuration appears to champion indiscriminate tolerance and a relative conception of truth. While this might speak to modern sensibilities, it is not what Maimonides truly had in mind. He regards truth as both narrowly defined and universal at the same time. Moreover, his words show him not only keenly aware of the prejudices his readers might entertain, but also willing to sacrifice scholarly ideals in order to circumvent those prejudices. If we wish to understand Maimonides' words properly, we must first consider what he means by "truth" and then look at his words in their original context.

Maimonides maintains that there is one truth conceived in various ways. The purest philosophical embodiment of this truth is Aristotelian philosophy as it has been systematized in late antiquity and elaborated in Arabic philosophy and science. This philosophy constitutes for Maimonides both the foundation and, to a certain extent, the culmination of the human quest for truth. If we seize this truth, we will not only perfect our intellect, we will also reach the ultimate goal of human existence: the contemplation of the one God.

Maimonides considers Aristotelian philosophy superior because it examines the world solely under the guidance of the intellect. This lack of preconceived notions distinguishes Aristotelian philosophy from intellectual endeavors Maimonides considers inferior. In particular, Maimonides rejects the approach taken by the proponents of rational theology, the *mutakallimūn*, in both Judaism and Islam. He claims that they, similar to their Christian predecessors, start from a particular religious doctrine they favor and then adduce whatever arguments they see best suited to establish this doctrine.

The fact that Maimonides rejects the approach of the theologians does not mean that he considers all religious texts to be false. Rather, the opposite is true. In his eye the prophets — chief among them Moses — are supreme philosophers. And since the prophetic texts are written by philosophers, they and the philosophical texts must convey the very same truth.

Yet prophets differ from philosophers. Maimonides seems to hold, first, that they have access to knowledge that philosophers cannot reach because true philosophical knowledge extends only about things up to the sphere of the moon. Moreover, prophets use their imagination to render the philosophical truth in a language their communities can understand. Because language changes, the literal meaning of the prophetic texts has come to differ from their philosophical intent. Readers of prophetic texts must, therefore, interpret these texts in such a way that they agree with the philosophical truth, whatever this truth might be. Maimonides even insists that, were the scientific truth to differ from the one we know, we would have to adjust our interpretation of the prophetic texts accordingly.

I should note here that Maimonides does not consider all prophetic texts to be equally valid, but gives clear preference to the Hebrew Bible. Not only does it precede all other prophetic texts in time, but it also comes closest to scientific truth. For example, a prophetic book that advocates the absolute oneness of God is much closer to Aristotle's ultimate cause than a religion which — in the eyes of Maimonides — strays from monotheism. Maimonides therefore considers Christianity to be farther away from the scientific truth than Judaism or Islam.

Regardless of which prophetic text comes closest to philosophical truth, one could read Maimonides' conception of truth in prophetic texts as purely elitist: On the one hand, we have those chosen few who understand the philosophical truth and are capable of interpreting the religious text accordingly; on the other hand we have those who are ignorant of the philosophical truth and live their lives according to a literal understanding of the prophetic texts.

While Maimonides thinks that human beings differ in their ability to grasp the philosophical truth, he does not sanction the literal understanding of prophetic texts as full alternative to the philosophical truth. In order to live a proper life and to reach ultimate happiness, every member of the religious community must — to the extent of his or her abilities — understand the philosophical truth of at least some aspects of the prophetic texts.

One aspect of prophetic texts Maimonides thinks all members of his religious community must interpret philosophically is its use of anthropomorphic language. When prophetic texts speaks of God in terms of a person that possesses a body, walks, perceives, speaks, and shows emotions, they clearly contradict the philosophical conception of the ultimate cause as a simple and immaterial entity. Would we allow people to adhere naively to the literal meaning of prophetic texts, we would lead them astray from the philosophical truth and, in the last consequence, from intellectual perfection and eternal bliss.

It is not difficult to imagine that the philosophical reading of prophetic texts advocated by Maimonides was rejected in some quarters of his religious community. Take, for example, questions concerning the doctrine of resurrection, which Maimonides accepts on the authority of the Jewish sources and includes as one of his famous principles of faith. Readers of his philosophical works doubted whether Maimonides truly accepted this doctrine and sparked a full-blown controversy that forced Maimonides to defend himself in writing. What led them to doubt Maimonides' sincerity is quite apparent even in the *Eight Chapters*. There Maimonides explains how the human rational soul can learn to renounce the distractions of its body and turn toward the knowledge of the first principle or God — its ultimate perfection. Such a philosophical anthropology seems indeed to have little use for the reconstitution of bodies at the end of days.

Much more should be said to properly appreciate Maimonides' conception of truth. But the little that has been said here sheds at least some light on what Maimonides had in mind when he asks us to "Hear the truth, whoever speaks it." And the precise context of his words, to which we now turn, adds yet another dimension worth considering.

Maimonides introduces his famous words by drawing our attention to the fact that his treatise, as well as the commentary it introduces, contains ideas he has collected from other sources, and that it lacks ideas of his own: "Know that what I say in these chapters and in the ensuing commentary are not ideas which I invented by myself, nor are they original interpretations. Rather, they are ideas gleaned from what the Sages say in the Midrashim, in the Talmud and elsewhere in their compositions, from what the philosophers say, both ancient and modern, as well as from the compositions of many other people: and you should hear the truth, whoever speaks it."[4]

Maimonides' words are not in themselves unique. One of the earliest proponents of philosophy in the world of Islam, Abū Yūsuf Ya'qūb al-Kindī (d. 873), who was himself a major patron of Graeco-Arabic translations, said in the introduction to his book on Metaphysics: "We ought not to be ashamed of appreciating the truth and of acquiring it wherever it comes from, even if it comes from races distant and nations different from us. For the seeker of truth nothing takes precedence over the truth, and there is no disparagement of the truth, nor belittling either of him who speaks it or of him who conveys it."[5] And even the Mishnaic tractate *Avot*, which Maimonides expounds in the commentary following the *Eight Chapters*, opens its fourth chapter with a statement by Simon Ben Zoma, a rabbinic authority of the second century CE, which bears some resemblance to Maimonides words: "Who is a wise person? He who learns from all men. For it is said 'From all my teachers I have learned understanding' (Psalms 119:99)."

But Maimonides goes beyond al-Kindī and the text of the Mishnah. For he uses his famous words to justify that in the *Eight Chapters* he will copy entire statements of the Sages and earlier philosophers without referring to his sources in the form of "so-and-so said." Maimonides justifies this suppression of references in two ways. First of all, he has already declared that he is merely the collector and not the creator of these ideas. If he were to supply references, he would add nothing to that declaration while prolonging the treatise.

In the second place, Maimonides claims that references can actually come as a detriment to some readers. Maimonides singles out those readers who judge a text not by its content, but immediately reject when its author turns out to be a person whose authority they do not accept. If Maimonides were to add references, he would be of disservice to those readers, since he would prevent them from benefitting from the truth contained in the texts he is quoting in the *Eight Chapters*.

4 Yosef Kapaḥ (ed.), Mishna 'im perush Rabbenu Moshe ben Maimon. Seder Neziqin. Jerusalem: Mossad Harav Kook 1965, pp. 372 f.

5 Kitāb al-Kindī ilā l-Mu'tasim bi-llah fī l-falsafa l-ūlā, in: Roshdi Rashed and Jean Jolivet (eds.), Œuvres philosophiques et scientifiques d'al-Kindi, vol. 2, Métaphysique et cosmologie, Leiden, Brill 1998, p. 13; translation taken from Alfred L. Ivry, Al-Kindī's Metaphysics. A translation of Ya'qub ibn Isḥāq al- Kindī's treatise "On First Philosophy" (fī al-Falsafah al-ūlā) with introduction and commentary, Albany, State University of New York Press 1974, p. 58.

One source from which Maimonides copies has been identified by scholars as the *Aphorisms of the Statesman* (*Fuṣūl al-Madanī*) by Abū Naṣr al-Fārābī (d. c. 950), a famous Muslim logician and philosopher. Maimonides greatly admired al-Fārābī's writings and recommended them to his students. We can easily imagine why Maimonides would have expected a person prejudiced against Muslim and Greek philosophy to reject quotations from a treatise written by a Muslim philosopher, a philosopher whose views on human perfection seem not only incompatible with a traditional outlook but also close to Aristotle's *Nicomachean Ethics*. Yet Maimonides considers these views essential to the message of the Mishnaic tractate *Chapters of the Fathers*, as demonstrated by the many references to parts of the *Eight Chapters* in his commentary on the Mishnah. He therefore chose to omit direct references to al-Fārābī in an attempt to help his reader accept the philosophical truth.[6]

Abstract
»Höre die Wahrheit, wer sie auch spricht«: Einleitende Bemerkungen zu Moses Maimonides und seiner Ermahnung

Der einleitende Beitrag bietet einen kurzen Überblick zu Leben und Werk von Moses Maimonides und diskutiert dessen Ermahnung »Höre die Wahrheit, wer sie auch spricht«. Es wird gefragt, was Maimonides mit Wahrheit meint und was seine Ermahnung in ihrem ursprünglichen Kontext bezweckt. Der Beitrag zeigt, dass sie eine unwissenschaftliche Praxis didaktisch rechtfertigt: Maimonides unterlässt es, seine nicht-jüdischen Quellen zu belegen, um zu verhindern, dass seine Leser die in ihnen enthaltene Wahrheit zurückweisen.

Lukas Muehlethaler is junior professor for Jewish philosophy and aesthetics at the Freie Universität Berlin and at the Center for Jewish Studies Berlin-Brandenburg. He studied Jewish intellectual history at the Hebrew University in Jerusalem and in 2010 received a PhD in Arabic and Islamic studies at Yale University with a dissertation on the Jewish philosopher Ibn Kammūna. Prior to his appointment he was part of the Research Unit Intellectual History of the Islamicate World at the Freie Universität Berlin. He works in the field of Jewish and Muslim intellectual history of the Middle Ages with a focus on the interaction between different intellectual and cultural traditions.

6 That Maimonides is indebted to al-Fārābī both in the content of his *Eight Chapters* as well as in the saying has been pointed out by Herbert A. Davidson in his superb study "Maimonides' 'Shemonah Peraqim' and Alfarabi's 'Fuṣūl Al-Madanī,'" Proceedings of the American Academy for Jewish Research 31, 1963, pp. 33–50.

Maribel Fierro

The Islamic West in the Time of Maimonides: The Almohad Revolution

► Al-Andalus ► Almohads ► Almoravids ► Berbers ► Dhimma ► Fatimids ► Ibn al-ʿArabī ► Ibn Rushd (Averroes) ► Ibn Ṭufayl ► Islamic legal schools ► Ismaʿiliyya ► Madrasa ► Mahdī ► Qibla ► Shia Islam ► Sufism ► Sunni Islam

After having studied previous centuries, anyone approaching the study of the 12th century in the Islamic West – the regions that are now Morocco, Algeria, Tunisia, the western part of Libya and al-Andalus (the Iberian Peninsula) – enters fascinating and somewhat unusual times. What helped to create a cultural milieu in which scholars seemed always to have felt obligated to think and say new things – or old things in new ways? I am referring to scholars such as Ibn Ṭufayl (ca. 1105–1185), Ibn Rushd/Averroes (1126–1198), Maimonides (1135–1204) and the famous mystic Muḥyī l-dīn Ibn ʿArabī (1165–1240). Of course, some scholars in preceding times shared some of the same intellectual concerns and strove to change habits of thought and ways of doing things they considered to be epistemologically misguided as well as culturally and religiously stifling.[1] But in the 12th century such efforts seem to have passed from the margins to the centre of attention, and they need to be understood within the cultural and religious policies of the Almohad caliphs. Such cultural and religious policies also influenced the intellectual project of Alfonso X (r. 1252–1284), king of Castile, whose father Fernando III had extended Christian rule to most of the territory of the former Almohad Empire. Alfonso X could be said to have been the "last Almohad caliph" in his complex religious, cultural and political projects, consisting of the promotion of new scholars, profound institutional and legislative reform, the direct involvement of the king in cultural policies with the objective of gaining encyclopaedic knowledge, a desire to extend education to the people at large, hence the use of the vernacular, and the flourishing of didactic literature. All this closely paralleled what the Almohad caliphs did.[2]

1 Ibn Masarra (d. 931), Ibn Ḥazm (d. 1056), and Ibn Gabirol (d. 1058) are some such scholars.

2 Maribel Fierro, Alfonso X 'the Wise', the Last Almohad caliph?, in: Medieval Encounters, 15 (2009), pp. 175–198.

The Almohad Revolution[3]

The Almohads did what revolutionaries do: They openly and explicitly marked the break between the old and the new times, often resorting to the use of violence, but also developing an ambitious propagandistic and pedagogical programme to habituate their subjects to the new Almohad beliefs and ways of doing things. They introduced substantial changes in political institutions, coinage, mosques, religious practices, and the world of religious scholarship, changes that came with specific visual and auditory presentations.

Almohad silver coins were minted in a square shape, while the dinar was circular with an inscribed square. These are shapes closely associated with the Almohads, as shown for example in their flags and also in their copies of the Qur'ān. Almohad coins carried no date, as if to indicate that a new era had begun. The new age was symbolised in the texts appearing on the coins, reminding Muslims that "God is our Lord, Muhammad is our Prophet, the Mahdi or Messiah is our *imām*", and that 'Abd al-Mu'min and his descendants were the new caliphs. The centre had clearly shifted from the East to the West.

Almoravid mosques were purified and their decorations destroyed or hidden. Attempts were even made to correct the orientation of some mosques. The call to prayer was made with new formulas, some of them in Berber. Differences of opinion (*ikhtilāf*) in the field of law were rejected, since there could only be one Truth. Jurists trained in the legal tradition hegemonic in the Islamic West, that of the Maliki legal school, were viewed with suspicion – at least in the early stages of the movement – and the Almohad caliphs tried to replace them with new personnel loyal to the new doctrines, the ṭalaba.[4]

These changes were made possible by the preaching of one man, the Masmuda Berber Ibn Tūmart (d. 1130), who is the Mahdī mentioned in the Almohad coins. His profession of faith (more on this below) constituted the kernel of the Almohad revolution, and everybody under Almohad rule was obliged to learn it by heart, be they Muslim, Jew or Christian. The teaching and explanation of its contents were entrusted to the members of the Almohad religious and political elites, the *ṭalaba*. In fact, the imposition of Ibn Tūmart's profession of faith – formulated by a 'rightly guided one' or Mahdī – was what al-

3 For a more detailed treatment of the issues dealt with here, see Maribel Fierro, The Almohad Revolution. Politics and Religion in the Islamic West During the Twelfth-Thirteenth Centuries, Ashgate, Variorum 2012; and most especially: Conversion, Ancestry and Universal Religion: the Case of the Almohads in the Islamic West (Sixth/Twelfth-Seventh/Thirteenth Centuries), previously published in: Journal of Medieval Iberian Studies, 2/2 (2010), pp. 155–174.

4 Émile Fricaud, Les ṭalaba dans la société almohade (le temps d'Averroés), in: Al-Qanṭara, 18 (1997), pp. 331–388.

lowed the first Almohad caliph to dismiss the existing religious elites and to substitute them with new personnel. The *ṭalaba* – a term meaning those who studied and therefore were learned – were recruited from the most promising young men to serve the Almohad political and religious cause in different capacities. Their recruitment started under 'Abd al-Mu'min, the Zanata Berber and follower of Ibn Tūmart, who eventually emerged as his successor after the Mahdī's death in 1130 and who, through his military conquests, was the *de facto* builder of the Almohad empire, stretching from Tunisia to al-Andalus.

Ibn Tūmart's Profession of Faith

Ibn Tūmart had taught his profession of faith in Berber to his followers, who were mostly Berbers. After 'Abd al-Mu'min expanded Almohad rule to new territories, the profession of faith had to be learned by everyone who became his subject. This was because it was claimed that it contained the one and only Truth, and that it was the Truth because it had been formulated by 'the impeccable leader and acknowledged rightly guided one'.

The term Almohads derives from *al-muwaḥḥidūn* (Unitarians), that is, those who believed in the unconditional unity of God. This was the main message contained in the profession of faith proclaimed by Ibn Tūmart, together with the rejection of anthropomorphism.[5] Different versions were prepared in order to make its contents accessible to different categories of people. The Almohads wanted to extend it as far as possible, as indicated by the fact that versifications of the Almohad profession of faith were made in order to facilitate its memorization.[6] As long as their rule lasted – from the times of 'Abd al-Mu'min until Marrakech surrendered to the Marinids in 1269 – Ibn Tumart's profession of faith circulated widely in the territories of the Almohad Empire.

The Almohad profession of faith[7] insists on God's unity, eternity, incommensurability and omnipotence. It states that God exists in an absolute man-

5 Delfina Serrano, ¿Por qué llamaron los almohades antropomorfistas a los almorávides?, in: Patrice Cressier/Maribel Fierro/Luis Molina (eds.), Los almohades: problemas y perspectivas, Madrid, CSIC/Casa de Velázquez 2005, vol. 2, pp. 451–476.

6 Henri Massé, La profession de foi (*'aqīda*) et les guides spirituels (*morchida*) du Mahdi Ibn Toumert, in: Mémorial Henri Basset, Paris 1928, vol. 2, pp. 105–121; Dominique Urvoy, Les professions de foi d'Ibn Tūmart. Problèmes textuels et doctrinaux, in: Los almohades, vol. 2, pp. 739–752.

7 What follows is taken from: Maribel Fierro, The Religious Policy of the Almohads, in: Sabine Schmidtke (ed.), The Oxford Handbook of Islamic Theology, Oxford, Oxford University Press forthcoming.

ner, that He is known by the necessity of reason, that He is the Creator of humankind, and that He as Creator of everything cannot be compared to His creation in order to avoid falling into anthropomorphism. Ibn Tūmart's profession of faith ends by stating that God will be seen on the Day of Judgement but without comparison or modality, and that the Prophetic mission is confirmed by miracles. It is unclear whether these last two sections were always part of the text. The Almohad movement was a revolution that underwent different stages, and in this process doctrines and the narrative of events were subject to change. In any case, the Almohad profession of faith is concerned with, and concentrates on, God and His unity. The treatment of prophecy, ritual, divine law and eschatology normally found in Islamic creeds is absent here, except for the above-mentioned reference to the vision of God in the afterlife and Muḥammad's miracles. The abbreviated versions (the *murshidas*) focus exclusively on God's unity and omnipotence. This strong emphasis on God's unity was theoretically acceptable to Jews as well, but not to the Christians, who according to the Muslims were responsible for the sin of dividing Divine unity into three parts (*tathlīth al-waḥdāniyya*)[8]. In his "Letter on Forced Conversion", addressed to the converted Jews of Almohad lands, Maimonides stated that "there has never been a persecution as remarkable as this one, where the only coercion is to say something".[9] What I am suggesting here is that the original version of the Almohad profession of faith may not have included any reference to the Prophet Muḥammad, so that it would have appeared even more acceptable to the non-Muslims. In any case, both Muslims and non-Muslims were in fact forced to convert to "Almohadism" as condensed in Ibn Tūmart's profession of faith.

While in the case of Muslims they were forced to renounce the pluralistic religious scenario of Sunnism for one specific interpretation of the message of Islam, in the case of Jews and Christians they had to renounce their religion altogether. But why demand such forced conversion that affected Maimonides among many other Jews in the Islamic West?[10] It is one of the most striking and puzzling decisions made in the early stages of the Almohad revolution, as it meant the abolishment of the *dhimma* status that had protected the Jews

8 This expression is taken from a 12th-century Muslim polemical work against Christianity: Thomas Burman, Tathlīth al-waḥdānīyah and the Twelfth-Century Andalusian Christian Approach to Islam, in: John Victor Tolan (ed.), Medieval Christian Perceptions of Islam: a Book of Essays, New York, Routledge/Chapman & Hall 1996, pp. 109–128.

9 Esperanza Alfonso, Islamic Culture through Jewish Eyes. Al-Andalus from the Tenth to the Twelfth Century, London/New York, Routledge 2008, pp. 106–107.

10 For a thoughtful discussion of a polemical episode in the life of Maimonides, see Joel L. Kraemer, Maimonides: the Life and World of One of Civilization's Great Minds, New York, Doubleday 2008, esp. pp. 116–124.

and Christians living under Muslim rule for centuries.[11] Five elements need to be taken into account in order to understand the religious, legal and political context that could have precipitated such an unprecedented policy:

a) *Eschatology*, the conviction that the appearance of the Mahdī would bring about the disappearance of religions other than Islam.
b) *The influence of Shi'i Isma'ili*, represented by the Fatimid caliph al-Ḥākim's persecution of the *dhimmīs*, which also has to be related to eschatology.
c) Influence of *the belief that all human beings possess an innate nature (fiṭra)* that corresponds to Islam, whereas being a Jew or a Christian depends on the family into which one has been born.
d) The idea that *the territory ruled by the Almohads was a new Ḥijāz*. In the same way that the Prophet Muḥammad forbade the presence of any religion other than Islam in the territory of the Arabian Peninsula – and more specifically in the Ḥijāz, where the sacred towns of Mecca and Medina were located – the Almohads may have thought that the same prohibition applied to the territory where the doctrines of their founder the Mahdī now reigned supreme.
e) The Almohads could have also been influenced by *the legal doctrine of the jurist al-Ṭabarī* (d. 923), according to which once demography had become favourable to the Muslims, they would no longer be in need of non-Muslims – and could therefore abolish the *dhimma* pact completely.[12]

In my view, what the Almohads did was purporting to have recovered the original monotheism from which Jews, Christians and Muslims had departed. Previous monotheists were not so much forced to convert to the new religion, but rather to "rediscover" their true innate nature, to return to their *fiṭra*. This would make sense of the reports that, in the first stages, the Almohads engaged in debates with the Jews in different localities in order to convince them of their religious truth and thus bring about their conversion.[13] The real emphasis was not so much on the fact that the Almohad Truth was a revival of the Prophet Muḥammad's message and of the Revelation brought to

11 On this event, see Jean-Pierre Molénat, Sur le rôle des Almohades dans la fin du Christianisme local au Maghreb et en al-Andalus, in: Al-Qanṯara, 18 (1997), pp. 415–414; Amira Bennison, Almohad *tawḥīd* and its Implications for Religious Difference, in: Journal of Medieval Iberian Studies, 2/2 (2010), pp. 195–216.

12 Maribel Fierro, A Muslim Land without Jews or Christians: Almohad Policies Regarding the "Protected People", in: Matthias M. Tischler/Alexander Fidora (eds.), Christlicher Norden – Muslimischer Süden. Ansprüche und Wirklichkeiten von Christen, Juden und Muslimen auf der Iberischen Halbinsel im Hoch- und Spätmittelalter, Münster, Aschendorff Verlag 2011, pp. 231–247.

13 Amira Bennison/María Ángeles Gallego, Jewish Trading in Fes on the Eve of the Almohad Conquest, in: Miscelánea de Estudios Árabes y Hebraicos. Sección Hebreo 57 (2008), pp. 33–51.

both Jews and Christians, but that it was identical with God's order or disposition (*amr Allāh*).[14] The Almohad Truth was the universal religion of mankind to which every human being had to adhere. This Almohad conviction had to do with their Messiah or Mahdī, an infallible *imām* who was the Rightly Guided One and the one who could lead others to the right path, but also with the stress that a certain trend within Almohadism placed on reason and on man's ability to perfect himself and reach a true understanding of God. I return to this point shortly.

To summarize, what the Almohads originally did was to force the population of the lands they had conquered to convert to what they viewed as the universal religion, one that could be reduced for the masses to a very basic understanding of God's unity and eternity – and one that had been brought to humankind by a man, Ibn Tūmart, endowed with infallibility. That basic faith was enough to save, a conviction that we can find also in Maimonides,[15] for whom proselytism had a symbolic value because it announced the return to original monotheism and hence was a sign of the imminent arrival of the End of Days.[16]

The Truth and Man's Access to It

While Ibn Ṭufayl's (d. 1185) close links with Almohadism are generally accepted,[17] the nature of such links in the cases of Averroes, Maimonides and Ibn ʿArabī has been the subject of varied interpretations. Underlying such interpretations seems to be a reluctance to accept the connection of three major intellectual figures who greatly influenced Christianity, Judaism and Islam in a Berber Muslim dynasty that is mostly associated with fanaticism and violence. Thanks to recent scholarship on the Almohads, it is slowly becoming more and more evident that they have to be acknowledged as having set in motion an exceptional and sophisticated political, religious and intellectual

14 Émile Fricaud, Origine de l'utilisation privilégiée du terme *amr* chez les Mu'minides almohades, Al-Qanṭara, 23 (2002), pp. 93–122; Salvador Peña, El término de origen coránico *amr Allāh* ("Disposición de Dios") y el linguocentrismo trascendente islámico, en torno al siglo XII, in: Anaquel de Estudios Arabes, 22 (2011), pp. 197–224.

15 In his "Letter to Hasdai Ha-Levi", he says that "There is no doubt that every man who ennobles his soul with excellent morals and wisdom based on the faith in God, certainly belongs to the men of the world to come … The basis of all things is (knowledge) that nothing is eternal save God alone …" English translation in: Isadore Twersky (ed.), A Maimonides Reader, New York, Behrman House 1972, pp. 477–478.

16 Alfonso, Islamic Culture through Jewish Eyes, p. 104.

17 Lawrence Conrad, An Andalusian Physician at the Court of the Muwaḥḥids: Some Notes on the Public Career of Ibn Ṭufayl, in: Al-Qanṭara, 16 (1995), pp. 3–14.

experience that changed the Islamic West, influenced the Islamic East in ways still to be fully explored, and most especially Latin Christendom and Judaism. Within this understanding, to accept the 'Almohadism' of Ibn Ṭufayl, Averroes, Maimonides and Ibn 'Arabī becomes less controversial, especially if we take into account that the second Almohad caliph, Abū Ya'qub Yūsuf (r. 1163–1184), initiated a move towards philosophy in order to overcome the limitations of Mahdism. Only then did Averroes start to write his commentaries on Aristotle with the caliph's backing, in order to make his philosophy more accessible.[18] Averroes was 'recommended' to the caliph by Ibn Ṭufayl,[19] the author of the extraordinary work "The self-taught philosopher", which he wrote during the reign of Abū Ya'qub Yūsuf, whom he served in various capacities.

Ibn Ṭufayl's work should be considered an Almohad text, even if it is in fact much more than that. One of the ways of reading this work is precisely as a political tract[20] that proposes how to advance the Almohad movement after the establishment of the empire, while also being alert to the limits of the revolution in terms of the truths available to different kinds of people.

The tale deals with a child who grows up on an island without any contact with other human beings and by the mere observance of nature and the reasoning of his intellect reaches both a philosophical and mystical understanding of God.[21] Later on, Ḥayy encounters a man, Absāl, who had grown up on another island where the inhabitants were followers of the teachings of a prophet. Absāl was interested in the allegorical interpretation of those teachings, and drawn as well to retirement and meditation, this being the reason he had originally arrived on Ḥayy's island. Absāl taught him to speak his language and then learned from Ḥayy how he had achieved knowledge of that Truth that he, Absāl, was striving to reach. Ḥayy and Absāl then decided to move to Absāl's island in order to teach that Truth to its inhabitants. They were ruled by Sālamān, a former friend of Absāl, who was also a scrupulous believer, but who was mostly interested in the literal meaning of the proph-

18 On this project, see Josep Puig, Averroes' Commentaries on Aristotle: To Explain and to Interpret, in: Gianfranco Fioravanti/Claudio Leonardi/Stefano Perfetti (eds.), Il commento filosofico nell'Occidente latino (secoli XIII–XV), Rencontres de philosophie médiévale 10, Turnhout, Brepols 2002, pp. 327–358.

19 Nemesio Morata, La presentación de Averroes en la corte almohade, in: La Ciudad de Dios 153, 1941, pp. 101–122. Sarah Stroumsa formulated some doubts about this "presentation" in: Philosophes almohades? Averroes, Maïmonide et l'idéologie almohade, in: Los almohades, pp. 1137–1162.

20 On Ibn Ṭufayl's political thought, see Hillel Fradkin, The Political Thought of IbnṬufayl, in: Charles Butterworth (ed.), The Political Aspects of Islamic Philosophy. Essays in Honour of Muhsin S. Mahdi, Cambridge, Harvard University Press 1992, pp. 234–261.

21 What follows reflects how I have benefited from the various contributions included in: Lawrence Conrad (ed.), The World of Ibn Ṭufayl. Interdisciplinary Perspectives on Ḥayy ibn Yaqẓān, Leiden, Brill 1996.

et's teachings. Soon, Ḥayy and Absāl realised that they could not change Sālamān's people – even that it was not desirable to change them – and therefore decided to return to their chosen isolation.

Ibn Ṭufayl's book teaches that not everyone can be a "unitarian" (*muwaḥḥid*), and that those who succeed will always be *ghurabā'*, i. e., strangers among the other believers. The majority, in fact, need what religion is there to offer them.[22] When Ḥayy was taught about religion by Absāl, he did not find any discrepancy between the prophet's teachings and what he had discovered on his own by means of reason. Nevertheless, he could not but wonder why that prophet had often used allegories in the description of the divine world, something that led men to anthropomorphism. Ḥayy's wonder was based on his belief that all men were endowed with penetrating intelligence. He soon learned that even Absāl's friends were unable to understand what he tried to teach, because they limited themselves to knowledge acquired through chains of authority. Ḥayy finally came to realize that there were different types of people, and that some of them needed the guidance found in the revelations received by prophets. True knowledge should not be taught to those incapable of understanding it. Another matter is to what extent their knowledge of religion itself can be improved, for example, whether the masses should be left to their anthropomorphic beliefs or whether they should be obliged to learn a correct creed.[23]

Ibn Ṭufayl's pupil Averroes was also a member of the Almohad *ṭalaba*, having written a commentary of Ibn Tūmart's creed and also a work explaining how he had been recruited by the Almohads and how he had entered the ranks of their scholars.[24] As is well known, Averroes described three different ways in which knowledge could be acquired: rhetorically, dialectically and philosophically. The philosopher cannot make philosophers out of everyone, in the same way that the doctor whose aim is "to preserve the health and cure the diseases of the people, by prescribing for them rules which can be commonly accepted"[25] is unable to make them all doctors. Averroes was, however, convinced that the masses should be better educated than they had been until then. He did not speak directly to the people, but in his theoretical writings he

22 Hayy ben Yaqdhân, Roman philosophique d'Ibn Thofaïl, Arab text and French translation by Léon Gauthier, 2nd edition, Beyrouth, Imprimerie Catholique 1936, p. 136/100.

23 Lawrence Conrad, Through the Thin Veil: On the Question of Communication and the Socialization of Knowledge in Ḥayy b. Yaqẓān, in: The World of Ibn Tufayl, pp. 244–245.

24 Maribel Fierro, Debating Again on Averroes and the Almohads, forthcoming, originally a paper presented at Marquette University (November 2011) and at the EHESS, Paris, 22 May 2012 (Séminaire de Pierre Bouretz). I wish to thank Prof. Richard Taylor and Prof. Maurice Kriegel for the opportunity to present my work and the debate that ensued.

25 Ibn Rushd/Averroes, Fasl al-maqal, transl. by George Hourani, Averroes on the Harmony of Religion and Philosophy, London, Luzac 1961, p. 22.

outlined "the manner in which the caliphs and the more learned classes of society should speak to them" and one "of the ways in which Ibn Rushd's commentary on the *Republic* differs from Plato's original is in the emphasis on the educational task of the ruler."[26]

Education and Encyclopaedism

Education was clearly a major concern of the Almohad revolution. If the Almohads wanted to change religious beliefs (anti-anthropomorphism) and practices, they had to extract people from their former beliefs and practices. In the early stages, the Almohads resorted to coercion and violence, but since the very beginning, they also used preaching and debates in order not to coerce, but rather to convince. After the initial impulse of the revolution, education seems to have become the prime target.

Ideally, the *ṭalaba* had to be able to engage in independent religious and legal reasoning, as servile imitation of late precedents (*taqlīd*) was censured. In connection with the need to train them, the Almohad caliphs promoted the production of encyclopaedic works collecting everything that was known at the time about a particular subject, as well as didactic works, often in versified form, and this in practically all disciplines.[27]

Non-coercive education of the masses had to be done by oral means, such as the public reading of caliphal letters, sermons and preaching. The Almohads had official preachers and promoted the writing and delivery of sermons. There is evidence of an increase in the production and circulation of Qur'ān copies. The dimensions of the square-formatted Almohad Qur'āns is an indication that the book was not perhaps meant to be a "pocket book", but rather was meant to facilitate its reading in diverse settings and perhaps its transportation. There is also more abundant information about copying activities.

All these transformations should be connected with the Almohad need to *educate the educators* entrusted with the spread of Almohad doctrines and practices. The Almohad promotion of the writing of didactic works often in

26 Charles E. Butterworth, New Light on the Political Philosophy of Averroes, in: Georges F. Hourani (ed.), Essays on Islamic Philosophy and Science, Albany, State University of New York Press 1975, 118–127, p. 125.

27 What follows is a summary of my forthcoming study "Education for the People? The Case of the Almohad Revolution", a paper presented at the Near and Middle East History Seminar, SOAS (London), 7 February 2011 and at the EHESS, Paris (Séminaire de Maurice Kriegel), 22 May 2012, as well as of a previous study in Spanish: "El saber enciclopédico en el mundo islámico", in: Las Enciclopedias en España antes de l'Encyclopédie, ed. Alfredo Alvar Ezquerra, Madrid, CSIC 2009, pp. 83–104.

versified form – leading to a production of didactic materials for which I do not find any parallel in previous periods – must have been directed to the training of the *ṭalaba* and *ḥuffāẓ*.

Of course, the use of didactic verse was not exclusive to the Almohads, given the crucial role of memorisation in Muslim teaching and scholarship. The popularity of didactic verse can be detected especially in the 13th century, although since the time the *madrasa* flourished throughout the Arabo-Islamic world, didactic versifications became a widespread instrument in the scholastic tradition. Under the Almohads we find versifications in almost every field, including Almohad creeds, medicine, the five pillars of Islam, mathematics, grammar …

The Almohad period experienced not only a flourishing of didactic verse, but also of encyclopaedism. Concern for compiling the extant knowledge in well-organised and user-friendly works can be detected – again – in almost every field: Qur'ānic exegesis, grammar, *adab*, medicine, botany, astronomy, agriculture, magic and so on. Averroes can be considered an encyclopaedist in the rational sciences,[28] and the same can be said of his contemporary Muḥyī l-dīn Ibn 'Arabī in the field of Sufism.[29] It is in Ibn Ṭufayl and in the more philosophically oriented of the Almohad intellectual elites that we find encyclopaedism at its best, that is, concern not only for compiling everything known until that moment of each discipline, but more importantly concern for establishing the general principles of those disciplines, as indeed Averroes and Maimonides did.[30]

Averroes openly directed his criticism against those jurists who were too attached to the opinions of their predecessors and thus measured knowledge by quantity, not quality, comparing them to shoemakers who accumulate huge quantities of shoes of different sizes but are incapable of making a shoe of the size required. All the authors mentioned so far (Ibn Ṭufayl, Averroes, Maimonides, Ibn 'Arabī) were interested in the principles of each discipline and not in casuistry. Behind this concern that produced the originality and depth found in their writings lies the impulse unleashed by the preaching

28 Charles E. Butterworth, In What Sense is Averroes an Encyclopedist?, in: S. Harvey (ed.) The Medieval Hebrew Encyclopaedias of Science and Philosophy, Leiden, Brill 2000, pp. 99–119.

29 Michel Chodkiewickz, Un océan sans rivage: Ibn Arabi, le livre et la loi, Paris, Editions du Seuil 1992.

30 Maribel Fierro, The Legal Policies of the Almohad Caliphs and Ibn Rushd's *Bidāyat al-mujtahid*, Journal of Islamic Studies 10/3, 1999, pp. 226–248; Sarah Stroumsa, Maimonides in his World: Portrait of a Mediterranean Thinker, Princeton, Princeton University Press 2009; Carlos Fraenkel, Legislating Truth: Maimonides, the Almohads and the Thirteenth Century Jewish Enlightment, in: Resianne Fontaine/Ruth Glasner/Reimund Leicht/Giuseppe Veltri (eds.), Studies in the History of Culture and Science. A Tribute to Gad Freudenthal, Leiden/Boston, Brill 2011, pp. 209–232.

of the Berber Ibn Tūmart, whose doctrine was described by one of the earliest non-Almohad sources at our disposal as a *madhhab fikr*,[31] a path of rational discovery.

Abstract
Die almohadische Revolution und ihre Auswirkungen auf die jüdischen Gemeinden des islamischen Westens

Die almohadische Revolution begann auf dem Gebiet des heutigen Marokko mit Ibn Tumart, der dem Berberstamm der Masmuda angehörte und als unfehlbarer Mahdi (Messias) galt. Einige Zeit nach Ibn Tumarts Tod im Jahr 1130 wurde sein Schüler Abd al-Mu'min – ebenfalls ein Berber, doch von einem anderen Stamm – sein Nachfolger und beanspruchte für sich den Titel »Fürst der Gläubigen«. Abd al-Mu'min war der Begründer des Almohadenreiches, das sich vom westlichen Libyen bis an die nordafrikanische Atlantikküste erstreckte und auch das muslimische Spanien (al-Andalus) umfasste.

Die Almohaden taten, was Revolutionäre zu tun pflegen: Sie markierten möglichst deutlich und oft gewaltsam den Bruch zwischen der alten und der neuen Zeit. Eine einschneidende Maßnahme der Almohaden war die Abschaffung der Dhimma, also des Rechtsschutzes für Andersgläubige unter muslimischer Herrschaft: ein fast beispielloser Schritt in der islamischen Geschichte. Tatsächlich wurden nicht nur Christen und Juden, sondern auch nicht-almohadische Muslime gezwungen, sich zur almohadischen Wahrheitsauffassung zu bekehren. Doch bald kam die Sorge auf, wie sich sicherstellen ließ, dass alle Zwangskonvertiten wirklich zu Rechtgläubigen geworden waren. Unter der Herrschaft des dritten Almohaden-Kalifen al-Mansur (1184–1198) wurde z. B. aus dieser Unsicherheit heraus den ehemaligen Juden eine spezielle, erniedrigende Art der Bekleidung vorgeschrieben.
Inwieweit wurde Maimonides' intellektuelle Ausbildung von der almohadischen Revolution beeinflusst?

Maribel Fierro is Research Professor at the Centre of Human and Social Sciences at the Higher Council for Scientific Research (CSIC – Spain). She has worked and published on the religious and intellectual history of al-Andalus and the Islamic West. Among her recent publications: "Abd al-Rahman III, The first Cordoban caliph", Oneworld, 2005; "Decapitation of Christians and Muslims in the Medieval Iberian Peninsula: narratives, images, contemporary perceptions", Comparative Literature Studies, 45/2 (2008), 137–64 and The Almohad revolution. Politics and religion in the Islamic West during the twelfth-thirteenth centuries, Variorum, 2012. She is the editor of volume 2 (The Western Islamic world, eleventh-eighteenth centuries) of the The New Cambridge History of Islam, Cambridge University Press, 2010.

31 Francesco Gabrieli, Le origini del movimento almohade in una fonte storica d'Oriente, Arabica 3, 1956, pp. 1–7, quoting the Eastern historian Ibn al-Qalānisī (d. 1160).

Sarah Stroumsa

Conversions and Permeability between Religious Communities

▸ Al-Andalus, Iberian Peninsula ▸ Almohads ▸ Judaeo-Arabic ▸ Midrash ▸ Nestorian Christians ▸ Sabians ▸ Sasanians ▸ Shia Islam ▸ Sunni Islam ▸ Zoroastrianism

Although the maxim chosen to welcome the visitors of this museum was coined, in this form, by Moses Maimonides, and although the principle which this maxim lays down guided Maimonides in all his intellectual endeavors, it is worth noting that his own works greet their reader with a different saying. The pious admonition Maimonides chose to open all his works with is neither "listen to the truth, whoever speaks it", nor the ubiquitous Jewish formula "*be-shimkha raḥmana*" ("in Your name, Oh Merciful One"), the most commonly used Jewish equivalent to the Muslim *Basmalah* in this period. What Maimonides chose was a formula that stems from the Biblical history of Abraham: "In the name of the Lord, God of the World" [Gen. 21:35]. Maimonides' deviation from the formulaic blessing, his recognizable personal touch on the opening of his works, turns the pious blessing into a motto, and draws our attention to Abraham and to the special place he held in Maimonides' thought. The patriarch's figure served Maimonides as a model, and central to this model was the fact that Abraham was a convert. We usually use the term "conversion" when a person abandons one religion and adopts another. Abraham, however, adopted the religion of "the God of the World", though he cannot be said to have abandoned his ancestral religion. According to both Jewish and Muslim tradition, Abraham never actually adhered to his father's religion. His conversion took place when he was still an infant, hiding from the wrath of King Nimrod. Sitting at the opening of the cave in which he was hiding, he observed the night and day replacing each other and contemplated the revolving heavenly bodies. In the span of 24 hours Abraham recognised that the planets are governed by a single and immaterial God – and thus became the first monotheist. Abraham's mental change, recounted in the Midrash as well as in the Qur'ān, is noted with admiration by Maimonides at the beginning of his legal codex, where he says: "He started roaming in his mind, when he was still little … and his heart was roaming and understanding."[1]

1 Moshe Ben Maimon, Mishneh Torah, Jerusalem, Levin-Epstein 1965, vol. 1, p. 56 (Sefer ha-mada', Hilkhot avodat kokhavim 1:3).

Maimonides, however, also puts great emphasis on Abraham's missionary program. Abraham's path began with a personal conversion, when he used his own judgment to attain true monotheism. But he then moved on to convert others, and his sustained proselytising effort eventually led to the demise of the dominant polytheism, which Maimonides identifies as the religion of the Sabians. Maimonides depicts Abraham as boldly and tirelessly spreading the word:

"... and he was traveling and preaching, and summoning people, going from city to the city and from kingdom to kingdom, until he reached the land of Canaan, where 'he called the name of the Lord, God of the World.'" [Gen. 21:35][2]

In Maimonides' eyes, Abraham thus triggers a gradual but irreversible train of conversions of global magnitude. In this gradual process, not only Judaism, but also Christianity and Islam prepare the way to the Messianic age, in which "the earth will be filled with the knowledge of the Lord, as the waters cover the sea" [Habbaquq 2:14]. For Maimonides, Abraham is the model for the development of the individual contemplative philosopher. At the same time, Abraham's spiritual trajectory also encapsulates and foretells the religious history of the world, and the religious progress of humanity as Maimonides saw it.

Maimonides constructs the figure of Abraham as the patron of converts to the true religion. He evokes Abraham's name when he wishes to encourage a proselyte who had been slighted,[3] and he relies on Abraham when he argues for the right of converts to say the prescribed blessing over the new fruits they bring to the Temple in Jerusalem. Relying on God's declaration to Abraham: "For I have made you the father of many nations" [Gen. 17:5], Maimonides states that the convert can and should pronounce the words: "as You have sworn to our fathers" [Deut. 26:3], "for Abraham is the father of all people, for he taught them religion."[4] The particular place which Maimonides accords to Abraham, the first true convert, may reflect his own experience with conversion, to which we will return below.

In Maimonides' figure of Abraham we can thus recognize two main kinds of conversion:

2 Ibid.

3 R. Moses b. Maimon, Responsa, Jehoshua Blau (ed.), Jerusalem, Mekize Nirdamim 1957–1986, vol. 2, p. 728.

4 Maimonides' Commentary on the Mishnah: Mishnah 'im Perush Rabbenu Moshe ben Maimon, Joseph Kapaḥ (ed.), Jerusalem, Mossad Ha-Rav Kook 1965, vol. 1, p. 417. See further: Sarah Stroumsa, The Father of Many Nations': Abraham in al-Andalus, in: Ryan Szpiech (ed.), Exegesis and Religious Difference: Essays on Commentary, Conflict, and Community in the Medieval Mediterranean, New York, Fordham University Press, forthcoming.

1) a personal religious or ideological transformation (like the one achieved by the infant Abraham), which may refer either to the move from one religion to another or to the change from no religiosity to deep religious feeling;
2) group religious transformation, usually a gradual process, where the religious change also results in a gradual general transformation – cultural, ethical, and communal – of the relevant society.

The notion of group conversion, with the ensuing cultural transformation, highlights the intrinsically dynamic and porous nature of human society, and the fact that dynamism and porosity are a precondition for such transformations. Quite often, new converts prove to be the most energetic and effective facilitators of cultural exchange. On the one hand, converts are sometimes fanatically devoted to their new religion, or feel obliged to appear as devout in order to be accepted by their new coreligionists. At the same time, even the most genuinely devout new converts continue to serve as repositories of their own original tradition, which, either purposefully or unconsciously, they may then transfer to their newly adopted culture.

A particularly complex and interesting case of intercommunal exchange facilitated by converts is presented by forced conversions, and it is to several aspects of forced conversions that I would like to devote the rest of this paper.

In the world of medieval Islam, forced conversions were not the rule, but rather an aberrant exception. Following the Qur'ānic pronouncements, practically all legal schools in Islam (both Sunni and Shi'i) allow Jews, Christians and, by extension, also Zoroastrians and at times Hindus to retain their religious identity, endowing them with a protected, albeit humble, status.[5] Notwithstanding this relative religious toleration, individuals belonging to these religions (which eventually became minorities in the world of Islam) sometimes found themselves in situations of duress, to which conversion to Islam seemed the most expedient solution. Although such conversions are not usually defined as "forced conversions", they were not motivated by strictly religious reasons, and in some cases they were clearly the result of some kind of coercion.

Historiographers record some instances of such coerced conversion regarding individuals who rose to high positions in the court in late antiquity or in the medieval world. Paradoxically, it is this elevated position that made them more vulnerable and thus exposed them to pressures to convert to the dominant religion. I will dwell here only on two such cases, from two different religious milieus. In the sixth century, in a cultural context that preceded the rise of Islam but had a major impact on the shaping of Islamic philosophy,

5 See Yohanan Friedmann, Tolerance and Coercion in Islam: Interfaith Relations in the Muslim Tradition, Cambridge, Cambridge University Press 2003.

Paul the Persian, a Nestorian Christian, attached himself to the court of the famous patron of philosophy Khosraw Anushirwān. The 13th-century author Barhebraeus claims that Paul "embraced Zoroastrianism because his ambition for ecclesiastical preferment was thwarted".[6] Another well-known example from a much later period is the twelfth century Jewish philosopher and physician Abū'l-Barakāt al-Baghdādī (d. 1165) who converted to Islam at a very old age. Our sources give several versions of the reasons for his conversion – accusations of malpractice, wounded pride or rivalry at court – but none of them suggests a spiritual experience that changed his religious views.[7]

In different ways these two cases demonstrate the precarious situation of the high official belonging to a minority group. Such officials struggled, on the one hand, with the need to keep a low profile regarding their original religion in order to maintain their position and, on the other hand, with the urge to remain faithful to their own cultural heritage and to continue to tap into it. It seems that, in order to satisfy this latter urge, these two authors, half a millennium and an empire apart, resorted to similar techniques. They were both deeply rooted in their own religious tradition: Paul the Persian served as a cleric in the Nestorian church, and Abū'l-Barakāt had written a philosophical commentary on the book of Ecclesiastes in Judaeo-Arabic. Both of them also wrote strictly philosophical compositions: a Syriac introduction to Aristotelian logics and commentaries on his work, by Paul the Persian; and a comprehensive philosophical book in Arabic, *al-Kitāb al-Muʿtabar*, by Abū'l-Barakāt. These philosophical works were ostensibly non-religious in character, and yet it is revealing to discover in both cases very clear Biblical quotations in translation, quotations that are unannounced and thus remain veiled to the non-Christian or non-Jewish reader. Abū'l-Barakāt includes in his work a quotation from Ecclesiastes 12:12, which can be seen as a nostalgic recall of his own commentary on this book.[8] Paul the Persian inserts in his introduction to Aristotle's logic verses from the book of Proverbs [8:19] and from Ecclesiastes [2:14], praising the wise man and wisdom in general.[9] These quotations show that, for Paul, Bible exegesis and logic are closely linked, and

6 Barhebraeus, Chron. Eccles., vol. 3, p. 97; and see Addai Scher (ed.), The Chronicle of Se'ert (Patrologia Orientalis VII.147), Paris 1911.

7 See Shlomo Pines, Studies in Abu'-Barakāt al-Baghdādī's Poetics and Metaphysics, in: Scripta Hierosolymitana 6, 1960, pp. 120–198 (reprinted in: The Collected Works of Shlomo Pines, vol. I, Jerusalem, Magnes 1979, pp. 259–334), on p. 121 (= 260), note 4.

8 Abū'l-Barakāt al-Baghdādī, al-Kitāb al-Muʿtabar, Haiderabad, 1358H, vol. 2, p. 437.

9 Jan Pieter Nicolaas Land (ed. and transl.), Anecdota Syriaca, Leiden, Brill 1875 (reprinted Jerusalem 1971), vol. 4, pp. 1 and 63. See further Sarah Stroumsa, Philosophy as Wisdom: On the Christians' Role in the Translation of Philosophical Material to Arabic, in: Haggai Ben-Shammai/Shaul Shaked/Sarah Stroumsa (eds.), Exchange and Transmission Across Cultural Boundaries: Philosophy and Science in the Mediterranean World, Jerusalem, The Israel Academy of Science and Humanities, 2013, pp. 276–293.

he passes on this Christian legacy to the Sassanian ruler. Surreptitiously, these two half-hearted converts thus transmit their own heritage to the dominant community and integrate this heritage into their adoptive culture.

Individual conversions under duress reveal the permeability of medieval culture in subtle, sometimes tantalisingly evasive ways. The picture is a lot clearer when we examine mass forced conversion. In the 12th century, the Almohads attempted to impose their idiosyncratic version of Islam on the countries under their rule, Islamic Spain and North Africa. Their revolutionary interpretation of Islam included Islamisation by force of the religious minorities. Although this ruling was not observed in all places and at all times with the same severity, Jews and Christians experienced it as a major trauma. While the conversions applied to both Jews and Christians, it seems to have been more effective among the Christians, whose communities virtually disappeared from North Africa. The Jewish communities proved more resilient, a fact that may explain the Almohads' somewhat harsher attitude towards Jews. In this context, a most telling testimony is that of al-Marrakushī, who states that under the Almohads there had been neither church nor synagogue in North Africa, but at the same time quotes the Caliph, who admitted to the possibility of an ongoing covert existence of Judaism.

One would expect forced conversion would have imposed the boundaries defining religious communities in a trenchant and simplified way: believers and infidels, "us" and "them". Paradoxically, however, the attempt to render these definitions more rigidly disturbed previous balances, created the necessity to wriggle around the boundaries and re-define them, and invented the techniques that enabled just such manoeuvres, while at the same time expediting processes of transmission of knowledge.

This is apparent even in the behavior of the coercing regime itself. The Almohads seem to have seriously attempted to cleanse the Iberian Peninsula of non-Muslims. One explanation for this policy is their wish to emulate Muslim sacred history and to apply the Muslim laws regarding the Arabian peninsula in the Iberian peninsula. Christian merchants or sailors were thus allowed to enter Almohad waters only to take refuge in times of clear hazard, such as stormy weather, and even then they were not allowed to dock. But in Almohad territory outside the peninsula, in North Africa, this policy was relaxed, and the merchants were allowed to step on shore.[10]

A quarter of a millennium later, the same double attitude can still be found in the policy of the Catholic Kings. The same king who expelled the Jews from

10 See Olivia Remie Constable, Trade and Traders in Muslim Spain: The Commercial Realignment of the Iberian Peninsula, 900–1500, Cambridge, Cambridge University Press 1994, p. 114.

Spain allowed them to establish a prosperous community in Oran, within Spanish territory.[11]

This flexibility, which allowed for some porosity in the presumably impenetrable wall of orthodoxy, is attested to mostly in trade documents, and mercantile activity was probably at the root of these cracks in that thick wall. Traders, however, carry not only palpable goods but also ideas. The forced conversions to Islam or to Christianity, which attempted to create a monolithic religious entity in the Iberian peninsula, also created a new kind of agent, who was able to pass through the pores of this new, apparently hermetically sealed society.

If the converting regimes themselves betray some permeability, the complexity of the situation created by forced conversions is naturally more in evidence in the writings of the converted people. When the opportunity presents itself for them to return to their previous religion, they lament what they experienced as their own shameful apostasy (as we can see in the poems of Isaac Ibn Ezra or in the writings of Maimonides), and express their complete repentance. Nevertheless, their religious identity continues to be treated with suspicion, by members of both their old and their new religious communities.[12] The suspicion may well be reinforced by the fact that by default these ex-converts carry with them some of the intellectual baggage of their previous religious identity, unwanted and forced upon them though it may have been. We thus find that, around the Mediterranean, these ex-converts tend to form their own closed communities.

The forced conversions of the Jews by the Almohads allowed for particular porosity, not only after those living as crypto Jews were able to return openly to their original faith, but already while they were under cover. Jews in North Africa were required to keep up Muslim appearances, but there was little surveillance. This is probably why Maimonides' family could move safely to Fes, close to the Almohad capital. Intellectually, the period of living as a crypto-Jew allowed Maimonides to move in and out of the Jewish and Muslim worlds. We thus find him integrating a Qur'ānic verse [Q. 59:2] into his *Guide of the Perplexed,* in the same way that Paul the Persian or Abū'l-Barakāt integrated Biblical verses into their philosophical work.[13] Maimonides' Jewish readers

11 See Jean-Frédéric Schaub, Les juifs du roi d'Espagne: Oran, 1507–1669, Paris, Le Seuil 1999.

12 See, for instance, Francesca Trivellato, The Familiarity of Strangers: The Sephardic Diaspora, Livorno, and Cross Cultural Trade in the Early Modern Period, New Haven and London, Yale University Press 2009, pp. 47, 53, 68–69.

13 The Guide of the Perplexed, vol. 2, p. 29 (Dalālat al-ḥā'irīn, Shlomo Munk and Issachar Joel (eds.), Jerusalem, 1931, p. 238); and see Warren Z. Harvey, Averroes and Maimonides on the Duty of Philosophical Contemplation (i'tibār), Tarbiz 58, 1989, pp. 75–83 [Hebrew].

would not have recognised the source, but its words became part and parcel of their own language.

Forced or coerced conversions, both individual and collective, thus introduced new and complex ways to address religiosity into the fabric of society, and they opened new channels for cultural exchange.

Instead of a conclusion, I wish to return to the half-hearted convert Abū'l-Barakāt al-Baghdādī, who, in his introduction to his philosophical book, says the following:

"[In this book] I did not aspire to adjust my opinions or the methods which I developed to those of great thinkers, because they are so great; nor to contradict the opinions of lesser thinkers, since they are less well known. My only purpose was to find the truth."[14]

A generation before Maimonides, we find Abū'l-Barakāt presenting the same openness and the same commitment to the truth, whatever its origin. Whether or not his belated conversion reflected this openness or perhaps enhanced it, it is clear that, among such scholars, the quest for truth was the dominant drive, sometimes more than their loyalty to the religion into which they were born.

Abstract
Konversionen und Durchlässigkeiten zwischen Religionsgemeinschaften

Das Konzept der Konversion – ob persönlich oder kollektiv – und die nachfolgende kulturelle Transformation bringen die wesenhafte Dynamik und Durchlässigkeit menschlicher Gesellschaften zum Vorschein. Gerade Neukonvertierte erweisen sich oft als die energischsten und erfolgreichsten Vermittler im kulturellen Austausch zwischen zwei Gesellschaften. Dieser Vortrag konzentriert sich auf erzwungene Konversionen und untersucht einige Aspekte ihrer komplexen Auswirkungen sowohl auf die Individuen als auch auf die Gesellschaft, in der sie leben. Im Mittelpunkt steht die Figur des Moses Maimonides, seine eigenen Erfahrungen unter den Almohaden und die Frage, wie sich diese Erfahrungen in seiner Haltung gegenüber Konvertiten widerspiegeln.

Sarah Stroumsa, the Alice and Jack Ormut Professor Emerita of Arabic Studies, teaches in the Department of Arabic Language and Literature and the Department of Jewish Thought at the Hebrew University, where she served as the Rector of the University from 2008 until 2012. Her area of academic focus includes the history of

14 Al-Kitāb al-Mu'tabar, vol. I, p. 4.

philosophical and theological thought in Arabic in the early Islamic Middle Ages, Medieval Judaeo-Arabic literature, and intellectual history of Muslims and Jews in Islamic Spain.

Among her published works are the following: The Beginnings of the Maimonidean Controversy in the East: Yosef Ibn Shimon's Silencing Epistle (Jerusalem: Ben Zvi Institute, 1999; Hebrew) Freethinkers of Medieval Islam: Ibn al-Rawandi, Abu Bakr al-Razi, and Their Impact on Islamic Thought (Leiden: Brill, 1999); and *Maimonides in his World: Portrait of a Mediterranean Thinker* (Princeton: Princeton University, 2010; Paperback edition 2012).

Gregor Schwarb

Eine maimonidische Trinitätslehre?

Zur Maimonidesrezeption in der koptisch-arabischen Literatur*

▸ Ayyūbiden ▸ Fatimiden ▸ Genisa ▸ Ibn al-ʿAssāl ▸ Kopten ▸ Mischna ▸ Rabbinisch ▸ Sabäer ▸ Zoroastrianism

Die Werke Maimonides': Sprache und Schrift

Maimonides schrieb seine philosophisch-theologischen Schriften in arabischer Sprache. Wie die meisten seiner jüdischen Zeitgenossen notierte er diese Texte in hebräischen Lettern. Sie richteten sich an jüdische Leser arabischer Muttersprache. In aller Regel handelte es sich dabei um Männer, die von Kindesbeinen an im Rahmen einer soliden religiösen Grundausbildung in die hebräische Schrift eingeführt worden waren. Die arabischen Schriftzeichen beherrschten sie dagegen oft nur passiv.[1]

Aus der Genisa der Ibn Ezra Synagoge in Fusṭāṭ-Miṣr (Alt-Kairo) und der Privatbibliothek seines Ururenkels David b. Joshuʿa (gest. 1415) in Aleppo sind uns von Maimonides mehrere Dutzend Holografen, d. h. Originalschriftstücke aus seiner Hand, erhalten geblieben.[2]

* Dies ist eine geringfügig überarbeitete Fassung eines am 9. Juni 2013 im Jüdischen Museum Berlin gehaltenen Vortrages. Eine detaillierte Darstellung der hier skizzierten Rezeption Maimonides' in der koptisch-arabischen Literatur findet sich in den folgenden Beiträgen: Gregor Schwarb, »Die Rezeption Maimonides' in der christlich-arabischen Literatur«. JUDAICA: Beiträge zum Verstehen des Judentums, 63 (2007), S. 1–45; ders., »The Reception of Maimonides in Christian Arabic Literature«. Y. Tobi (Hg.), Ben ʿEver la-ʿArav: Contacts between Arabic Literature and Jewish Literature in the Middle Ages and Modern Times. Volume 7: Maimonides and His World: Proceedings of the Twelfth Conference of the Society for Judaeo-Arabic Studies, Haifa: The University of Haifa, 2014, S. 109–175.

1 Judith Olszowy-Schlanger, Learning to Read and Write in Medieval Egypt: Children's Exercise Books from the Cairo Geniza, in: *Journal of Semitic Studies,* 48, 1 (2003), S. 47–69.

2 Colette Sirat/Silvia Di Donato, Maïmonide et les brouillons autographes du Dalâlat al-ḥâ'irîn (Guide des Égarés). Paris 2011; Solomon David Sasson, A Comprehensive Study of the Autograph Manuscript of Maimonides' Commentary on the Mishnah, Jerusalem 1990; Simon Hopkins, A New Autograph Fragment of Maimonides's Epitomes of Galen (De Locis Affectis), BSOAS 57, 1994, S. 126–132.

Abb. 1: Holograf (Schriftstück in Maimonides' eigener Handschrift) eines Entwurfs des »Führers der Unschlüssigen«, Teil I, Schluss des Kapitels 64 und Anfang des Kapitels 65 (Quelle: Cambridge University Library, T–S 10Ka4.1, f. 1v)

Einen Spezialfall bilden die medizinischen Werke Maimonides'. Auch diese hat er in arabischer Sprache und hebräischer Schrift verfasst. Einige davon entstanden jedoch als Auftragsschriften für Exponenten der muslimisch-ayyūbidischen Obrigkeit in Kairo und mussten so vor der Übergabe an den Auftraggeber von einem speziell für solche Zwecke ausgebildeten Schreiber der jüdischen Gemeinde in die arabische Schrift transponiert werden. Diese Schriften zirkulierten gewissermaßen von Geburt an in nichtjüdischen Kreisen.

Wie aber kam es, dass auch die arabischen Originale seiner nicht-medizinischen Schriften und insbesondere seiner religionsphilosophischen Haupt-

Abb. 2: Titelseite einer Abschrift des Führers (»Führer der Unschlüssigen und Wegmarkierung für jene, die unterwegs sind« – Kitāb Dalālat al-ḥā'irīn wa-talḥīb manāhiǧ as-sā'irīn) in der Handschrift des jemenitischen Zayditen Muḥammad b. Ḥasan al-Nihmī, Ṣa'da (Jemen), 882–3 A.H./1477–9 C.E. (Quelle: Istanbul, Jārullāh [Efendi] 1279, f. 189v. Foto © Süleymaniye Yazme Eser Kütüphanesi, Istanbul)

schrift »Dalālat al-ḥā'irīn« (»Führer der Unschlüssigen«) von nicht-jüdischen (christlichen und muslimischen) Lesern rezipiert werden konnten? Ein Erklärungsansatz ist wohl bekannt: Mehrere Dokumente belegen, dass schon sehr bald nach der Vollendung des Textes im Jahre 1190 Handschriften in arabischer Schrift im Umlauf waren.

Bis vor kurzem ist die Möglichkeit einer nichtjüdischen Rezeption des »Führers der Unschlüssigen« an die Existenz solcher Abschriften in arabischer Schrift geknüpft worden. Ein alternativer Erklärungsansatz, wonach

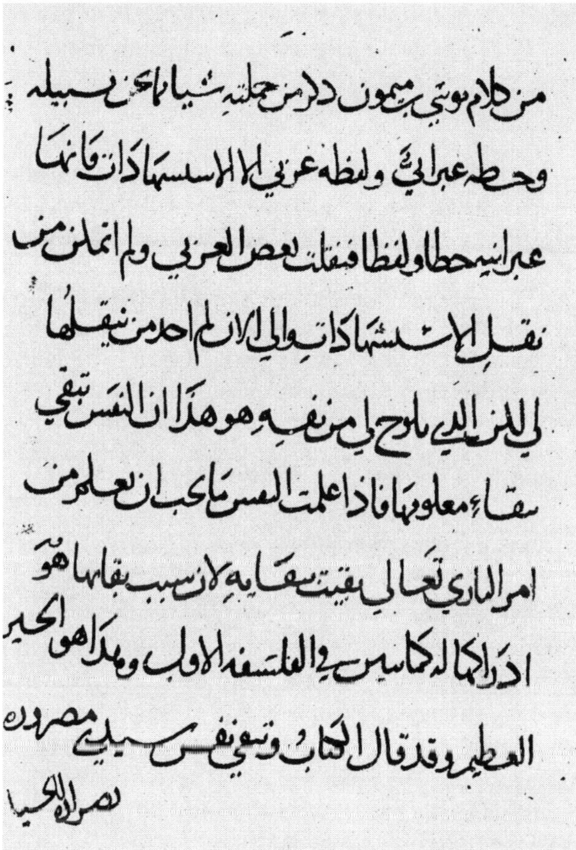

Abb. 3: Ausschnitt aus dem »Traktat über die Seele« (April–Mai 1231) des Kopten al-As'ad Abū l-Farağ Hibatullāh (gest. vor 1259) mit einem Zitat aus Maimonides' Kommentar zum zehnten Kapitel (Pereq Ḥeleq) des Mischna-Traktats Sanhedrin (Quelle: Vatican, Biblioteca Apostolica Vaticana, arab. 145, f. 4v. Foto © 2014 Biblioteca Apostolica Vaticana)

es durchaus auch nichtjüdische Leser gab, die in ausreichender Weise mit dem hebräischen Alphabet vertraut waren, um arabische Texte in hebräischer Schrift lesen zu können, wurde in der bisherigen Forschung als äußerst unwahrscheinlich verworfen. Interessanterweise führt uns jedoch genau dieses Szenario zum frühesten bisher bekannten Beleg einer christlich-arabischen Rezeption Maimonides'.

Er findet sich in einem noch unveröffentlichten »Traktat über die Seele« aus dem Jahre 1231, der in einem Unikat der Biblioteca Apostolica Vaticana vorliegt (Ar. 145). Al-As'ad Abū l-Faraj Hibatullāh Ibn al-'Assāl, der Autor dieser kleinen Schrift, entstammte einer einflussreichen Familie der koptischen Aristokratie im ayyūbidischen Kairo. In der Einleitung, in der er die ihm geläufigen Auffassungen über die Seele typologisch klassifiziert und zusammenfassend darstellt, schreibt er:

»Was die Juden betrifft, so begegnete ich im Jemen einem rabbinischen Juden und beobachtete, wie er sich über jene lustig machte, die an die Auferstehung aller Toten glaubten; dabei gäbe es doch im Alten Testament mehrere Textstellen, deren Wortsinn deutlich mache, dass nur rechtschaffene Menschen auferstehen würden. Zudem bin ich auf einen Text gestoßen, der Mūsā b. Maimūn (Maimonides) zugeschrieben wird, und Dinge betrifft, die zu unserem Thema gehören. Dieser Text ist in hebräischer (Schrift), jedoch in arabischer Sprache geschrieben, mit Ausnahme der Schriftzitate, deren Sprache Hebräisch ist. Ich habe einen Teil des arabischen Textes (in die arabische Schrift) transkribiert, war aber außerstande, die hebräischen Schriftzitate (ins Arabische) zu übersetzen und habe bisher auch niemanden gefunden, der sie für mich übersetzen würde.«

Bei besagtem Text, den der koptische Gelehrte offenbar während einer Reise in den Jemen zu Gesicht bekam, handelt es sich nicht etwa um einen Abschnitt aus dem »Führer der Unschlüssigen«. Vielmehr transkribierte er einen Ausschnitt aus Maimonides' berühmtem und ebenfalls auf Arabisch verfassten »Kommentar zur Mischna«, jener Schrift also, der auch der Wahlspruch der Akademie des Jüdischen Museums Berlin – »Höre die Wahrheit, wer sie auch spricht« (*wa-sma' al-ḥaqq mimman qālahu*) – entnommen ist.

Im selben Traktat über die Seele berichtet Ibn al-'Assāl auch von Gesprächen mit jemenitischen Juden. Diese hatten ihn auf eine Passage in einem Sendschreiben aufmerksam gemacht, welches Maimonides vierzig Jahre zuvor, also im Jahre 1191, an die jüdischen Gemeinden im Jemen gerichtet hatte.

Die Passage ist der berühmten »Abhandlung über die Auferstehung der Toten« (*Risāla/Maqāla fī teḥiyyat ha-metim*) entnommen, die Bestandteil eines über Jahre anhaltenden Prestigekampfes zwischen Maimonides und Samuel b. 'Elī, dem Vorsteher der alten jüdischen Akademie in Bagdad, war. Letzterer hatte Maimonides der Leugnung der körperlichen Auferstehung bezichtigt, da diese in der »Mischne Tora« unerwähnt bleibt.

Die koptisch-arabische Kulturblüte des 13. Jahrhunderts

Al-As'ad Ibn al-'Assāl, der Autor des »Traktats über die Seele«, gehörte, wie gesagt, einer prominenten Familie koptischer Geschäftsleute und Regierungsbeamter an. Die 'Assāliden und weitere koptische Familien, welche in der

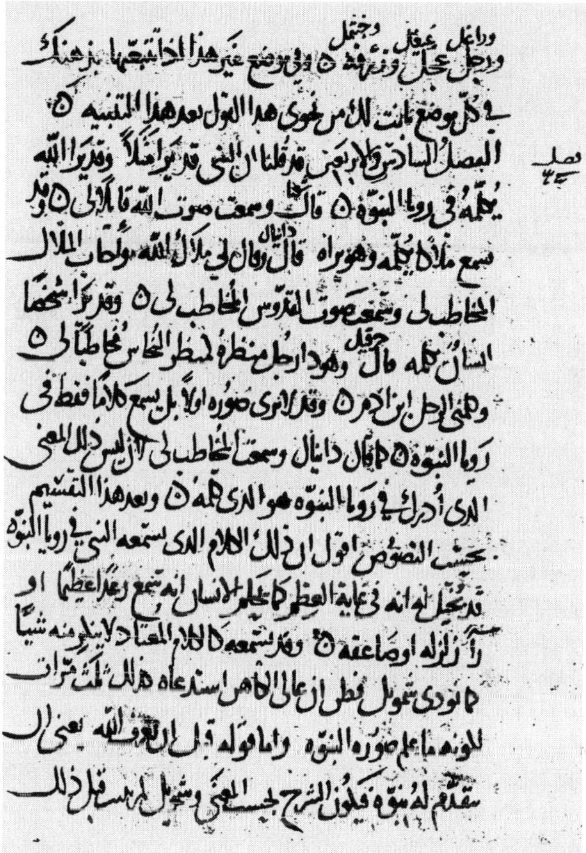

Abb. 4: Ausschnitt aus einer koptischen Kurzfassung des »Führers der Unschlüssigen«, Teil II, Ende des Kapitels 43 und Anfang des Kapitels 44 (Ende des Kapitels 45 und Anfang des Kapitels 46 gemäss der koptischen Zählung) (Quelle: Paris, Bibliothèque Nationale de France, arab. 205, f. 121v. Foto © BnF)

fāṭimidischen und ayyūbidischen Staatsadministration über mehrere Generationen hohe Ämter bekleidet hatten, waren Mäzene und treibende Kraft der im 13. Jahrhundert einsetzenden koptisch-arabischen Kulturblüte. Al-Asʿad Ibn al-ʿAssāl und andere machten sich einen Namen als Bibliophile und Handschriftensammler. Zahlreiche Dokumente und Handschriftenkolophone belegen, dass sie keinen Aufwand scheuten, um an Abschriften seltener Texte heranzukommen. Insbesondere in Kairo, Alexandria und Damaskus entstanden zwischen 1220 und 1270 mehrere bedeutende Privatbibliotheken, deren Bestände nicht nur arabische Texte der diversen christlichen Gemeinschaften, sondern auch zahlreiche Werke namhafter jüdischer und muslimischer Autoren umfassten.

Es darf in diesem Zusammenhang daran erinnert werden, dass die Arabisierung der koptischen Literatur und des koptischen Klerus erst gegen Ende des 12. Jahrhunderts abgeschlossen war. Zwar gab es bereits im 8. Jahrhundert christliche Beamte, deren Zwei- oder Dreisprachigkeit (Griechisch-Koptisch-Arabisch) für die Funktionsfähigkeit der neuen muslimischen Verwaltungsadministration unverzichtbar waren; solange aber die koptischen Christen die klare Bevölkerungsmehrheit stellten, gab es keinen zwingenden Grund, die beiden bestehenden Kultursprachen (Griechisch und Koptisch) zugunsten der arabischen Schriftsprache aufzugeben.[3]

Die Arabisierung der ägyptischen Christen war ein langwieriger Prozess mit großen regionalen Unterschieden. In den städtischen Zentren geschahen die entscheidenden Entwicklungen im 11. und 12. Jahrhundert, als die koptische Sprache kontinuierlich an Boden verlor und größere Bestände koptischer Texte ins Arabische übersetzt wurden.

Der Abschluss dieser Übergangsphase war gleichzeitig Voraussetzung der koptisch-arabischen Kulturblüte und ihrer eigenständigen Rezeption der arabischen Bildungsliteratur, zu der auch die Werke jüdischer und muslimischer Autoren gehörten.

Die Rezeption der Schriften Maimonides' durch koptische Autoren des 13. Jahrhunderts war also Bestandteil einer umfassenderen kulturellen Öffnung, die sich unter anderem in der Aneignung einer neuen philosophisch-theologischen Diktion manifestierte.

Gelegentlich führte diese aufgeschlossene Haltung auch zu intensiven persönlichen Kontakten zwischen christlichen und jüdischen Gelehrten. Auch vereinzelte Übertritte gebildeter Juden zum koptischen Christentum hatten im Laufe des 13. Jahrhunderts zu einem verstärkten Kulturaustausch beigetragen.

Ar-Rašīd Abū l-Ḫayr Ibn aṭ-Ṭayyib

Zu den Exponenten der koptischen Kulturblüte im 13. Jahrhundert gehörte auch Abū l-Ḫayr Ibn aṭ-Ṭayyib. Er lebte in Damaskus, wo er als koptischer Priester, Arzt und Privatsekretär eines georgischen Christen wirkte. Einige wenige Dokumente mit Informationen zu seiner Person weisen darauf hin, dass er als spitzzüngiger Querdenker und Autor umstrittener Pamphlete wiederholt in Konflikt mit den politischen Behörden und der kirchlichen Obrigkeit geriet.

3 Arietta Papaconstantinou (Hg.), The Multilingual Experience in Egypt, from the Ptolemies to the Abbasids. Farnham, Ashgate 2010.

Seine beiden Hauptwerke, welche für die koptische Rezeption der Schriften Maimonides' besonders interessant sind, können in die Zeit zwischen 1240 und 1260 datiert werden:

1) Das Gegengift der Vernunft im Bereich der Fundamentaltheologie oder die Enthüllung der dem Christentum zugrunde liegenden verborgenen Geheimnisse (*Tiryāq al-ʿuqūl fī ʿilm al-uṣūl al-musammā bi-Kašf al-asrār al-ḫafīya min asbāb al-Masīḥīya*)
2) Die Quintessenz des christlichen Glaubens und die Widerlegung der beiden Religionsgemeinschaften Islam und Judentum anhand ihrer Grundsätze und Fundamentallehren (*Ḫulāṣat muʿtaqad al-milla al-masīḥīya wa-'l-radd ʿalā ṭā'ifatay 'l-Islām wa-'l-Yahūdiyya min mawḍūʿātihim wa-uṣūl maḏāhibihim*).

Beide Werke, deren Edition der Autor dieser Zeilen zur Zeit vorbereitet, verfolgen ein ähnliches Ziel:

In der Einleitung zum »Gegengift der Vernunft« schreibt Abū l-Ḫayr:

»Mein Schirmherr und Gönner hat mich gebeten, für ihn eine kleine Abhandlung über die Grundlagen der Religion zu schreiben, in welcher die Glaubensgrundsätze der diversen christlichen Konfessionen dargestellt und deren Aussagen zur christlichen Glaubenswahrheit bewiesen werden sollen. Er hat mich zudem gebeten, mich zu einigen Punkten zu äußern, nach denen sich ein Repräsentant der muslimischen Obrigkeit erkundigt hatte, der gerne verstehen möchte, was die Christen mit der Formel ›Einheit der Substanz und Dreiheit der Hypostasen‹[4] meinen und wie es zulässig sein könne, dass Christus (dem Messias) das Attribut der Göttlichkeit beigefügt wird, wo doch die Indizien seiner Menschlichkeit so deutlich und klar seien. – Ich habe seinen Anweisungen Folge geleistet und alles mir Mögliche getan, um seinem Wunsch zu genügen.«

Gemäß der Einleitung zur zweiten Schrift, der »Quintessenz des christlichen Glaubens«, soll sich eine Gruppe muslimischer und jüdischer Gelehrter mit der Bitte an ihn gewandt haben,

»all das festzuhalten, was er zum Wesenskern des christlichen Glaubens an einen Schöpfergott sagen kann, und zu erklären, was die Christen mit der Glaubensformel ›Einer ist er‹ (*innahu wāḥid*[un]) meinen, wenn sie doch gleichzeitig die Formel ›der Vater, der Sohn und der Heilige Geist‹ verwenden, und wie es für Christen akzeptabel sein könne, Christus das Attribut der Göttlichkeit beizufügen, wo er doch ein Mensch sei, gebo-

4 *tawḥīd al-ǧawhar wa-taṯlīṯ al-aqānīm* < μία οὐσία, τρεῖς ὑποστάσεις. Gemeint ist die trinitarische Formel, welche die kappadozischen Väter im späten vierten Jh. in Erwiderung auf die Doktrin des Neo-Arianers Eunomius von Cyzicus entwickelt hatten und welche dem miaphysitischen Glaubensbekenntnis der syrisch-orthodoxen und koptischen Kirche zugrunde liegt.

ren von Maria, deren Genealogie wohl bekannt ist, und einer, der gemäß ihren eigenen Aussagen gegessen und getrunken hat, hungrig und durstig war, festgenommen und inhaftiert wurde, Schmerzen litt und gestorben ist, und so weiter und so fort.«

Die beiden Werke Ibn aṭ-Ṭayyib's ähneln sich nicht nur in ihrer Zielsetzung, sondern auch in ihrer Struktur. Einige Kapitel der »Quintessenz« sind wenig mehr als Kurzfassungen der Parallelkapitel im »Gegengift der Vernunft«. Beide Werke beginnen mit einem Kapitel zur christlichen Auffassung des Schöpfergottes. Ibn aṭ-Ṭayyib zufolge stimmt diese im Wesentlichen mit jener der Juden und Muslime überein. Diese Sichtweise wird dadurch verdeutlicht, dass sich das Kapitel weitgehend aus Zitaten jüdischer und muslimischer Werke zusammensetzt.

Die darauffolgenden Kapitel behandeln all jene Aspekte der christlichen Doktrin – Schriftzitate und theologische Lehrsätze –, welche die im ersten Kapitel verfochtene Einheit Gottes scheinbar beeinträchtigen: die trinitarische Formel, die Unvereinbarkeit von Christi Göttlichkeit und Menschlichkeit, Vaterschaft und Sohnschaft Gottes, Inkarnationslehre, die Vorstellung eines leidenden Gottes, und so weiter.

Den Grund dieser vermeintlichen Widersprüche erkennt Abū l-Khayr einerseits in der semantischen Unterbestimmtheit und Mehrdeutigkeit der christlichen Offenbarungstexte und andererseits im kulturellen Hintergrund der Adressaten dieser Texte. In der Einleitung zur »Quintessenz des christlichen Glaubens« betont er ausdrücklich, diese Erklärungsansätze in Büchern muslimischer und jüdischer Gelehrter gefunden zu haben, allen voran Faḫr ad-Dīn ar-Rāzī (st. 606/1210) und Maimonides.

Die Legitimität und Rationalität der christlichen Lehre ließe sich also mit Argumenten beweisen, deren Gültigkeit auch von den größten Lehrautoritäten des Judentums und des Islams bestätigt worden sei. Besonderes Gewicht wird dabei dem maimonidischen Akkommodationsprinzip beigemessen, wie es im dritten Teil des »Führers der Unschlüssigen« entwickelt wird.

Das maimonidische Akkommodationsprinzip

Im »Gegengift der Vernunft« und in der »Quintessenz des christlichen Glaubens« zitiert Abū l-Ḫayr längere Passagen aus den Kapiteln 26–49 des dritten Teils des »Führers der Unschlüssigen«, wobei nicht alle Zitate als solche gekennzeichnet sind. In diesen Kapiteln erklärt Maimonides Zweck und Funktion der gesetzlichen Bestimmungen der Tora aus den historischen Bedingungen und pädagogischen Bedürfnissen der ursprünglichen Adressaten, denen der gesetzgebende Gott in seiner gnädigen Klugheit Rechnung trug. In dieser

›göttlichen Pädagogik‹ erkannte Maimonides die sekundäre Absicht der *lex dei*, während ihre eigentliche, primäre Absicht auf die Abschaffung der Idolatrie und die Erkenntnis Gottes abzielte.

Das Rational der göttlichen Pädagogik liegt nach Maimonides darin begründet, dass für Menschen eine abrupte und unvermittelte Abkehr von tief verwurzelten Angewohnheiten, Grundhaltungen, Gesinnungen oder Überzeugungen unmöglich sei. Der Mensch sei von Natur aus unfähig, seine Gewohnheiten auf einen Schlag aufzugeben. Deshalb, so fährt Maimonides fort, sei es das Ziel sämtlicher Gebote und Verbote, schritt- und stufenweise auf die Unterbindung der Idolatrie und all dessen hinzuwirken, was mit ihr in Verbindung steht, zu ihr hinführt oder ihr zugeschrieben werden kann. Der offensichtliche Nutzen der Gebote bestehe darin, den Menschen sukzessive von jenen ungesunden Praktiken und Ideen zu befreien und damit das Erreichen seines körperlichen und seelischen Idealzustandes zu fördern.

»Die Bedeutung vieler Gebote und der Grund ihrer Legislation wurde mir durch das Studium der Lehren, Meinungen und Praktiken der Sabäer einsichtig. Du wirst verstehen, was ich meine, wenn ich die Gründe jener Gebote erläutern werde, von denen gemeinhin angenommen wird, dass es keinen Grund für sie gibt. Ich werde Dich auf die Bücher hinweisen, aus denen Dir alles ersichtlich werden wird, was ich über die Lehren und Meinungen der Sabäer weiß, so dass Du Dich vergewissern kannst, dass das, was ich als Gründe für diese Gebote anführen werde, korrekt ist.«

Auf dieses Verständnis der Religionsgeschichte greift nun Abū l-Ḫayr Ibn aṭ-Ṭayyib zurück, um die Legitimität und Rationalität der christlichen Glaubenslehre im Allgemeinen und der Trinitätslehre im Besonderen zu beweisen.

»Nachdem Du nun gehört hast, wie sehr die Christen auf der Einheit und Einzigkeit Gottes bestehen und davon absehen, ihm Eigenschaften der körperlichen Welt zuzuschreiben, solltest Du alles daran setzen, die befremdenden Beschreibungen Gottes, die in den Offenbarungstexten zu finden sind, zu verstehen, denn Gott ist weise und der Weise schafft nichts Nutzloses. […] Worin also liegt die Weisheit und die kluge Lenkung, ein Gesetz (*šarīʿa*) zu erlassen, durch welches alle Völker dazu bewogen werden, Gott zu verehren, indem sie Ihn mit verwerflichen Ausdrücken und befremdlichen Attributen beschreiben, wie etwa, wenn er zu den Aposteln sagt: ›Geht hin und macht alle Völker zu Jüngern; tauft sie auf den Namen des Vaters und des Sohnes und des Heiligen Geistes‹ (Mt 28,19) und nicht etwa: ›Tauft sie im Namen des einen, einzigen Gottes, von dem es nicht mehr als einen geben kann‹?«

Die Antwort auf diese Frage besteht nach Abū l-Ḫayr darin, dass das offenbarte Gesetz göttliche Lenkung und göttliche Führung sei, »welche die Menschen dazu bewegt, die Existenz des Schöpfers zu bejahen, jedes Volk mit (den Mitteln), durch die es Gewohnheit hat, sich Gott aus freien Stücken zuzuwenden.«

Seines Erachtens richten sich die neutestamentlichen Schriften an drei verschiedene Gruppen von Adressaten: 1) die Anhänger der griechischen Philosophie, 2) die Anhänger Zarathustras (Zoroasters) und 3) die Sabäer. Bis auf wenige Ausnahmen kann die gesamte Menschheit diesen drei epistemischen Paradigmen zugeordnet werden. Für jede dieser drei Wissensformationen hat die göttliche Weisheit ein angemessenes Gegengift (*Tiryāq*) bereitgestellt, welches sie der Erkenntnis des wahren Gottes näher bringen soll.

Wie Maimonides nennt Abū l-Ḫayr nun einige Bücher, aus denen er sein Wissen über die drei Religionstypen bezogen hat. Während Maimonides die »Nabatäische Landwirtschaft« als seine wichtigste Quelle hervorhebt, sind es bei Abū l-Ḫayr die pseudo-aristotelischen Hermetica und insbesondere der »Kitāb al-Isṭamāṭīs«, die als zentrale Referenzschriften ausgewiesen und ausführlich zitiert werden.

In diesen Büchern sei er unter anderem auf die Trinitarier (al-muṯalliṯa), eine Gruppe von Sabäern, gestoßen, die den Schöpfergott als Geist der Himmelssphäre bezeichnen, aus dem der Intellekt und die Seele hervorgegangen seien, die beide zur einen Substanz des Schöpfergottes gehören. Sie hätten deshalb an jedem Kultort drei Tempel gebaut. Die trinitarische Formel der christlichen Offenbarung sei ein durch göttliche Weisheit bewirktes Gegengift gegen solcherlei Vorstellungen und Praktiken entwickelt worden. Während vorchristliche Offenbarungen und insbesondere die Tora ausschließlich auf Gottesvorstellungen reagierten, die auf Sinneswahrnehmung beruhten, sei die christliche Offenbarung als Gegengift gegen falsch konzipierte philosophisch-universalistische Gottesbegriffe und damit verbundene Kultpraktiken zu verstehen.

»So richtet sich die Einleitung zum Evangelium des Johannes an die Bewohner von Ephesus, zu denen bekanntermaßen die führenden Köpfe der Sabäer, ihre Gelehrten und Philosophen gehörten, die (dort) ihre Kultstätte hatten. Deshalb führte Gott sie zu einer ihren Bedürfnissen angemessenen Lebensform hin, durch die sie zu wahrer Erkenntnis gelangen konnten. Diese Lebensform zöge insbesondere Verhaltensweisen in Betracht, die auf sie attraktiv wirkten, damit sie sich nicht abwenden würden. Aus diesem Grund beginne das Johannesevangelium wie folgt: ›Im Anfang war das Wort […]‹.«

Ähnliches gilt für den Brief des Paulus an die Bewohner der Stadt Kolossai. Kolossai sei eine Stadt der Sabäer und ein Hort der Philosophen gewesen. Sie hätten das Fundament ihrer religiösen Praxis so beschrieben, dass aus der *causa causarum* ein erster Intellekt überströmte und dass alle existierenden Dinge aus dem ersten Intellekt hervorgingen. Ihrer Lehre nach stehe es dem besagten Intellekt zu, zusammen mit der ersten Ursache und der Seele verehrt zu werden, wie es in ihren Glaubensgrundsätzen festgehalten wurde.

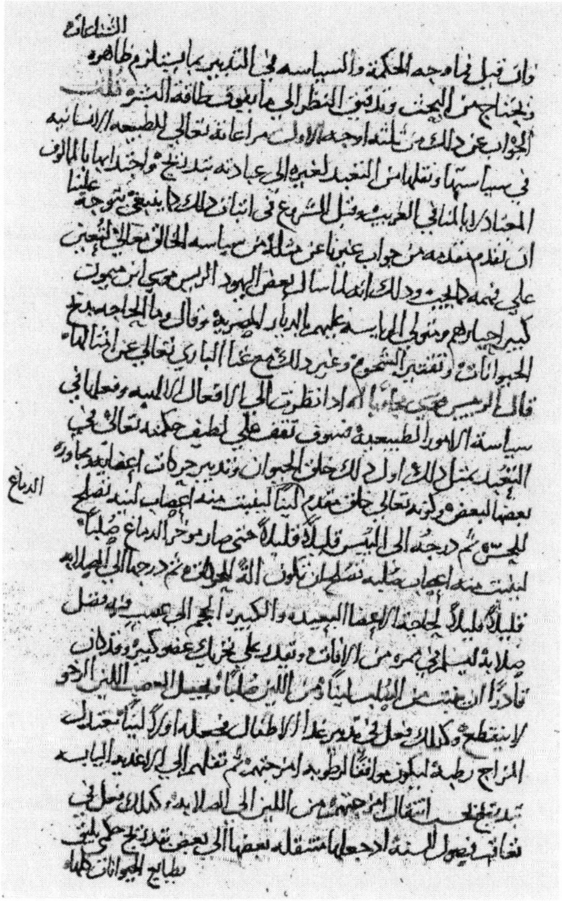

Abb. 5: Ausschnitt aus der »Quintessenz des christlichen Glaubens« des Kopten ar-Rašīd Abū l-Ḫayr ibn aṭ-Ṭayyib mit dem Beginn eines längeren Zitats aus Maimonides' »Führer der Unschlüssigen«, Teil III, Kapitel 32 (Quelle: Vatican, Biblioteca Apostolica Vaticana, arab. 105, f. 72r. Foto © 2014 Biblioteca Apostolica Vaticana)

Abū l-Ḫayr legte grossen Wert darauf zu betonen, dass seine Anlehnung an das maimonidische Konzept des religionsgeschichtlichen Fortschritts nicht als Abhängigkeit missverstanden werden soll. So beschließt er die »Quintessenz des christlichen Glaubens« mit den Worten:

»Merke wohl, der Du dieses Buch einsiehst, dass ich den Verfasser des *Führers* – der ja die jüdische Lehre vertritt – in den bisherigen Ausführungen nicht deshalb zitiert habe, weil es unentbehrlich war oder weil ich unfähig wäre, etwas Gleichwertiges zu schreiben, sondern um jenen Angehörigen der jüdischen Religionsgemeinschaft entgegenzutreten, die sich auf ihn berufen, damit ihnen durch die Aussagen des wichtigsten Vertreters ihrer Religionsgemeinschaft klar wird, dass die christliche Religion mit den göttlichen Absichten im Bereich der geistlichen Dinge und rationalen Methoden übereinstimmt, und damit ihnen klar wird, dass die gesetzlichen Einzelbestimmungen der Tora nicht um ihrer selbst willen erlassen wurden, sondern um hinzuführen auf das vollkommene Gesetz, das nach ihr kommt, damit sie dies begreifen und dementsprechend handeln. Zudem wurde dieses gesamte Buch nur als Antwort auf die Frage von Muslimen und Anhängern der jüdischen Religionsgemeinschaft geschrieben, die nach dem christlichen Gottesglauben (wörtl. »nach der Überzeugung der Christen von Gott«) fragten, so dass es sich anbot, gegen die Anhänger der beiden Religionsgemeinschaften das anzuführen, was ihre wichtigsten Exponenten gesagt haben, um ihnen damit entgegenzutreten.«

Außerdem verweist der Kopte auf vergleichbare Konzepte in Werken der Kirchenväter, beispielsweise den Begriff συγκατάβασις, der ab dem späten 4. Jh. in den Schriften Chrysostomos' und der kappadozischen Väter Verbreitung fand. Der Begriff ist der späthellenistischen Rhetorik entlehnt und bezeichnet die Anpassung (oder »Herablassung«) des Redners an das Niveau der Zuhörerschaft.

Diese knappe Darstellung zweier Werke des koptischen Gelehrten Abū l-Ḫayr ibn aṭ-Ṭayyib sollte hinlänglich gezeigt haben, dass die christliche Rezeption Maimonides' mitnichten auf den lateinischen Maimonides reduziert oder mit ihm gleichgesetzt werden kann. Dass Maimonides über die Stoßrichtung der christlich-arabischen Rezeption seiner Werke erfreut gewesen wäre, darf bezweifelt werden. Wie jedoch Sokrates in einer berühmten Passage des »Phaidros« (275 A) richtig festgestellt hat, entzieht sich der einmal niedergeschriebene Text der Kontrolle des Autors und treibt sich überall herum, gleichermaßen bei denen, die ihn verstehen, wie auch bei denen, die ihn missverstehen. Wie im vorliegenden Fall kann die Produktivität einer Wirkungsgeschichte durchaus auch aus dem absichtlichen Missverstehen eines Textes hervorgehen. In diesem Sinne möchte ich diese kurzen Ausführungen zur koptisch-arabischen Rezeption des Maimonides' mit einem leicht abgewandelten Nietzsche-Zitat beschließen: »Wir dürfen es tragen, falsch zu verstehen, um mehr zu sehen als da ist«.

Abstract
A Maimonidean Trinitarianism? On the Reception of Maimonides in Copto-Arabic Literature

Even though Maimonides' philosophico-theological works were written for Jewish readers, they aroused the interest of several exponents of Copto-Arabic literature during its 'Golden Age' in the thirteenth and fourteenth centuries. This little-known Christian-Arabic reception of Maimonides is presented by the example of two works by the Coptic theologian Abū 'l-Khayr Ibn al-Ṭayyib written around 1250 in Damascus. The Copt availed himself of Maimonides' concepts of 'divine wisdom' and 'divine pedagogy', according to which the revelation of religious knowledge accommodates itself to the historical conditions and educational needs of the respective audience. Based on this 'principle of accommodation', Abū l-Khayr developed his historical explanation of the Christian doctrines of incarnation and trinity, and thought he could thus prove the rationality and superiority of the Christian faith.

Gregor Schwarb studierte Theologie, Philosophie und Judaistik in Freiburg (Schweiz), Jerusalem und Damaskus. Bevor er 2009 als wissenschaftlicher Mitarbeiter zur Research Unit Intellectual History of the Islamicate World an der Freien Universität Berlin stieß, war er akademischer Direktor des Centre for the Study of Muslim-Jewish Relations in Cambridge. Als Experte für vormoderne arabische Geistesgeschichte arbeitet er schwerpunktmäßig zu Querverbindungen zwischen jüdischer, christlicher und islamischer Religionsphilosophie.

Lukas Muehlethaler

Al-Tabrīzīs Kommentar zu Maimonides' »Führer der Unschlüssigen«

Zur Maimonidesrezeption in der islamisch-arabischen Philosophie

▸ al-Baghdādī ▸ Ibn Bājja ▸ Crescas, Chasdai ▸ al-Fārābī ▸ Ibn Rushd (Averroes) ▸ Ibn Sīnā ▸ Tibboniden, Samuel ibn Tibbon

Wir sind weit davon entfernt, die Rezeption von Maimonides' theologischem und philosophischem Hauptwerk »Dalālat al-ḥā'irīn« (»Führer der Unschlüssigen«) in der islamisch-arabischen Philosophie vollständig zu überblicken.[1] Bisherige Forschung hat sich vor allem mit der Rezeption der hebräischen und lateinischen Übersetzungen beschäftigt, und die Erforschung der späteren islamisch-arabischen Philosophie steckt noch in ihren Anfängen.[2] Es besteht aber kein Zweifel daran, dass Maimonides' »Dalāla« von muslimischen Philosophen gelesen wurde.

Der Bericht des ʻAbd al-Laṭīf al-Baghdādī

Bereits zu Maimonides' Lebzeiten fand die »Dalāla« erste muslimische Leser. Ein berühmtes Beispiel ist der aus Bagdad stammende Arzt und Philosoph ʻAbd al-Laṭīf al-Baghdādī (gest. 1231/2),[3] der im Jahr 1191 auf einer Studienreise

1 Einen ausgezeichneten Überblick über die bisherige Forschung verschafft der Appendix in Gregor Schwarb, The Reception of Maimonides in Christian-Arabic Literature, in: Yosef Tobi (Hg.), Maimonides and His World, Haifa 2014, S. 143–46.

2 Die bisherige Forschungsgeschichte und ihre methodologischen Probleme erläutert Dimitri Gutas, The Heritage of Avicenna: The Golden Age of Arabic Philosophy, 1000–ca. 1350, in: Jules Janssens/Daniel De Smet (Hg.), Avicenna and His Heritage, Leuven 2003, S. 81–97.

3 Für neuere Arbeit zu ʻAbd al-Laṭīf al-Baghdādī siehe Cecilia Martini Bonadeo, ʻAbd Al-Laṭīf Al-Baġdādī's Philosophical Journey: From Aristotle's Metaphysics to the »Metaphysical Science«, Leiden 2013.

Kairo besuchte. Dort wollte er, unter anderen, Maimonides treffen. Ob dieses Treffen zustande kam, ist nicht klar. In seiner Autobiografie zeichnet ʻAbd al-Laṭīf zwar ein positives Bild von Maimonides (Mūsā ibn Maimūn al-Yahūdī), kritisiert in seiner scharfzüngigen Art aber zwei Dinge: Maimonides' Streben nach weltlicher Anerkennung und sein Werk »Dalālat al-ḥā'irīn«. Er bezeichnet es als ein »Buch für die Juden« und behauptet, dass Maimonides darauf bestanden habe, dass das Buch nur in hebräischer Schrift abgeschrieben werde. ʻAbd al-Laṭīf erhielt trotzdem Einblick in den Inhalt der »Dalāla« – ob in hebräischer oder arabischer Schrift lässt er offen – und stellte fest, dass es die Grundlagen des Religionsgesetzes und des Glaubens zerstöre, anstatt sie, wie von Maimonides beabsichtigt, wiederherzustellen.[4]

Die Randnotizen des Muḥammad ibn Ḥasan al-Nihmī

Sehr viel genauer und in arabischer Schrift hat Muḥammad ibn Ḥasan al-Nihmī Maimonides' »Dalāla« gelesen. Al-Nihmī lebte in der zweiten Hälfte des 15. Jahrhunderts im Jemen. Als Privatgelehrter und Liebhaber von Büchern sammelte er interessante Bände und schrieb sie gelegentlich zum eigenen Gebrauch ab.

In Istanbul wird eine von al-Nihmī zusammengestellte Sammelhandschrift aufbewahrt,[5] in der sich auch eine vollständige Abschrift von Maimonides' »Dalāla« in arabischer Schrift findet. Dass al-Nihmī dieses Werk sorgfältig gelesen hat, zeigen seine ausführlichen und detaillierten Randnotizen, die manchmal zustimmend oft aber auch kritisch ausfallen.

Al-Nihmī liest Maimonides' »Dalāla« im Kontext der arabischen Philosophie des 15. Jahrhunderts. So ärgert er sich zum Beispiel über Maimonides' Kritik an der Astrologie. Er lehnt auch Maimonides' Haltung zur Ewigkeit der Welt ab: Viele arabische Philosophen vertraten mit den aristotelisch-neuplatonischen Philosophen die Ansicht, die Welt sei ewig; Maimonides dagegen argumentiert in der »Dalāla«, dass es dafür keinen demonstrativen Beweis gebe. Ja, Aristoteles habe einen solchen nie beabsichtigt, und weil diese Frage also nicht abschließend bewiesen sei, schlägt Maimonides vor, dem Bericht der prophetischen Schriften zu folgen. Al-Nihmī weist Maimonides'

4 Ibn Abī Usaibiʻa (gest. 1270) zitiert eine Version von ʻAbd al-Laṭīfs Autobiografie in »Uyūn al-anbā' fī ṭabaqāt al-aṭibbā«, wo die hier besprochene Passage erscheint (Ed. Beirut 1965, S. 687).

5 Diese Handschrift (Carullah 1279) beschreibt Franz Rosenthal in »From Arabic Books and Manuscripts V: A One-Volume Library of Arabic Philosophical and Scientific Texts in Istanbul«, in: Journal of the American Oriental Society, 75 (1955), S. 14–23.

Auffassung zurück und behauptet, dass es sehr wohl gültige Beweise für die Ewigkeit der Welt gebe.[6]

Der Kommentar des al-Tabrīzī

Neben ʿAbd al-Laṭīfs allgemeiner Einschätzung der »Dalāla« aus dem 12. Jahrhundert und al-Nihmīs detaillierten Randnotizen aus dem 15. Jahrhundert gibt es auch einen Teilkommentar aus dem 13. Jahrhundert. Er stammt aus der Feder von Abū ʿAbdallah Muḥammad b. Abī Bakr b. Muḥammad al-Tabrīzī (st. 1278). Al-Tabrīzī war Arzt, Astronom und Philosoph und lebte im Osten der islamischen Welt.[7]

Der Kommentar von al-Tabrīzī beschränkt sich auf die Einleitung zum zweiten Teil der »Dalāla«, welche Maimonides mit einer Liste von sechsundzwanzig philosophischen Prämissen (*muqaddamāt*) eröffnet. Diese Prämissen sind notwendig, sagt Maimonides,

> »um die Existenz der Gottheit zu begründen und um demonstrativ zu beweisen, dass sie [d. h. die Gottheit] weder ein Körper noch ein Vermögen in einem Körper ist, und dass sie, erhaben sei ihr Name, eins ist.«[8]

In Maimonides' Liste finden sich kurze Prämissen, wie die erste: »Die Existenz einer unendlichen Größe ist unmöglich,« und längere, wie zum Beispiel die fünfzehnte:

> »Zeit ist ein Akzidenz, welches durch Bewegung entsteht und notwendig mit ihr verbunden bleibt. Keines kann ohne das andere existieren. Bewegung existiert nur in der Zeit und Zeit kann der Intellekt nur zusammen mit Bewegung erfassen.«

Die sechsundzwanzigste Prämisse, nämlich die Ewigkeit der Welt, hält Maimonides (wie oben erwähnt) für nicht demonstrativ beweisbar und gewährt sie den Philosophen nur unter Vorbehalt.

6 Al-Nihmīs nur schwer lesbare Randnotizen werden derzeit von mehreren Forschern untersucht und versprechen, unser Verständnis der Maimonidesrezeption in der späteren arabischen Philosophie zu erweitern. Eine erste Auswahl aus al-Nihmīs Randnotizen bieten Y. Tzvi Langermann/Almog Kasher, Critical Notes of Muḥammad bin Ḥasan al-Nihmī to Maimonides' Guide [hebr.], Daat 74–75, 2013, S. 237–266. Sie streben eine Gesamtedition der Randnotizen an.

7 Zu Tabrīzī siehe al-Kawṯarīs Einleitung zur Edition des Kommentars (siehe unten, Anm. 9), S. 22 f.

8 Salomon Munk/Issachar Joel (Hg.), Maimonides, Dalālat al-ḥā'irīn, Jerusalem 1929, S. 165. Die Liste der Prämissen endet auf S. 167.

An der Gültigkeit der ersten fünfundzwanzig Prämissen besteht laut Maimonides kein Zweifel; Aristoteles und seine Nachfolger hätten, so schreibt er, für jede Prämisse einen demonstrativen Beweis vorgebracht (d. h. einen Beweis, dessen Grund zwingend richtig und dessen Form logisch korrekt ist.) Maimonides ist sich seiner Sache derart sicher, dass er diese Beweise nicht aufführt, sondern lediglich eine Liste nackter Prämissen präsentiert.

Stellt jemand eine lange Liste angeblich bewiesener Prämissen vor, ohne die Beweise anzuführen, muss er damit rechnen, dass jemand diese Liste genauer betrachtet. Dies gilt besonders für die arabische Philosophie des 13. Jahrhunderts.

Im 13. Jahrhundert ist Philosophie nicht mehr einer kleinen Gruppe von Spezialisten vorbehalten. Philosophische Methoden der Argumentation gehören vielmehr zum Rüstzeug eines jeden Intellektuellen: Argumente müssen logisch korrekt und, wenn möglich, demonstrativ formuliert sein. Auch Argumente früherer Denker werden nach diesen Kriterien überprüft und vervollständigt. Aus diesem Grund sind Philosophen des 13. Jahrhunderts fasziniert von jenen Texten ihrer Vorgänger, die prägnant formuliert sind und nach solcher Verifikation (*taḥqīq*) verlangen.

Dass al-Tabrīzī zu dieser Tradition gehört, zeigt sich sowohl in der Methode seines Kommentars als auch in dessen philosophischen Inhalten. Sie stehen in der Nachfolge des berühmten muslimischen Philosophen Avicenna (Ibn Sīnā, gest. 1037). Er hatte im 13. Jahrhundert im Osten der islamischen Welt einen mit Aristoteles' vergleichbaren Status erreicht und prägte auch muslimische Theologen, wie z. B. Faḫr al-Dīn al-Rāzī (gest. 1210).

Maimonides erwähnt Avicenna zwar und übernimmt Elemente avicennischer Philosophie, doch er hat seine philosophische Bildung im muslimischen Spanien, in Nordafrika und in Ägypten erhalten: Seine großen Vorbilder sind muslimische Philosophen wie Abū Naṣr al-Fārābī (gest. 950–1), Ibn Bājja (gest. 1139) und vielleicht sein Zeitgenosse Averroes (Ibn Rushd, gest. 1198). Über allen thront Aristoteles, der vollkommenste aller Philosophen.

Al-Tabrīzīs Kommentar ist letztlich also auch eine avicennische Verifikation und Interpretation der von Maimonides präsentierten Prämissen.

Er eröffnet seinen Kommentar mit folgenden Worten:

»Abū ʿAbdallah Muḥammad b. Abī Bakr b. Muḥammad al-Tabrīzī sagt: Dies ist derjenige Teil aus dem Buch, welches wir kommentieren und erklären wollen, d. h. das Buch namens Führer der Unschlüssigen, in welchem der große Meister (*al-šayḫ al-ra'īs*), der weise, einzigartige, außerordentliche und vollkommene Abū ʿImrān Mūsā b. ʿUbaydallah al-Isra'īlī al-Qurṭubī [d. h. Maimonides] die möglichen Wege [oder: Methoden] anordnet, die zum wahren Wissen über den edelsten Teil der erhabensten Weisheit und zur ersten Philosophie führen, welche ihre höchste Bestimmung und ihr höchstes Ziel ist. Wenn die Seele des Menschen diese erreicht, wird die Substanz seiner Seele ähnlich der Substanzen der Engel, und sein Geist nähert sich der Stufe der Geister der himmlischen Sphären, wie es Dir, so Gott will, der Text dieses Buches bezeugen wird.«[9]

Ich möchte zwei Punkte dieser Passage hervorheben: Zum einen zeigt sie, dass al-Tabrīzī Maimonides voller Hochachtung begegnet. Der Beiname *al-šayḫ al-ra'īs* ist gewöhnlich der Beiname Avicennas. Zum anderen macht die Passage deutlich, dass Tabrīzī den Titel von Maimonides' »Dalālat al-ḥā'irīn«, d. h. »Führer der Unschlüssigen« als eine Metapher für den Zweck und das Ziel der fünfundzwanzig Prämissen interpretiert.

Für al-Tabrīzī sind Maimonides' Prämissen systematisch angeordnete Pfade hin zu Wissen über die Metaphysik. Al-Tabrīzī setzt bei dieser Interpretation Avicennas Verständnis vom Gegenstand der Metaphysik voraus.[10] Ihm zufolge ist Metaphysik nicht nur die Untersuchung von Sein qua Sein. Der erhabenste Teil der Metaphysik ist erste Philosophie, zu welcher unter anderem die philosophische Theologie gehört, und durch das Studium der Metaphysik erreicht die menschliche Seele ihre absolute Vollkommenheit. Diese Vollkommenheit ist doppelt: Zum einen wird der menschliche Intellekt den himmlischen Intellekten ähnlich. Zum anderen nähert sich die menschliche Seele den Seelen der Himmelssphären an. Dies alles vermittelt den Eindruck, dass al-Tabrīzī die fünfundzwanzig Prämissen nicht bloß als eine Einleitung zum zweiten Teil der »Dalāla« versteht, sondern in ihnen die Essenz des ganzen Buches sieht.

Al-Tabrīzīs Kommentar zur einundzwanzigsten Prämisse Maimonides'

Wir können uns hier keinen Überblick über al-Tabrīzīs gesamten Kommentar verschaffen. Ich habe mich deshalb entschlossen, den kürzesten Abschnitt aus al-Tabrīzīs Werk vorzustellen, seinen Kommentar zur einundzwanzigsten Prämisse von Maimonides.

Maimonides' einundzwanzigste Prämisse beruht auf Konzepten, die Avicenna in seiner Metaphysik entwickelt hatte. Avicenna unterscheidet in den Dingen zwischen ihrer Essenz und ihrer Existenz. Die Essenz ist, was das Ding ausmacht, seine »Washeit«, also zum Beispiel »Flusspferdehaftigkeit«.

9 Muḥammad Zāhid al-Kawṯarī (Hg.), Abū 'Abdallāh Muḥammad b. Abī Bakr b. Muḥammad al-Tabrīzī, Sharḥ al-Muqaddamāt, Kairo: Al-Maktaba al-azhariyya li-l-turāṯ 1993², S. 26.

10 Zu Avicennas Verständnis vom Gegenstand der Metaphysik siehe Amos Bertolacci, Avicenna and Averroes on the Proof of God's Existence and the Subject-Matter of Metaphysics, Medioevo, 32 (2007), S. 61–97.

Die Essenz existiert nicht als solche. Sie erhält ihre Existenz quasi als Akzidenz, wenn sie entweder in unserem Intellekt oder in der konkreten Realität zu existieren beginnt. Deshalb ist die Existenz eines Flusspferdes aus sich selbst nur möglich, notwendig ist sie durch eine andere Ursache. In letzter Konsequenz ist diese Ursache der einzig notwendig aus sich selbst Existierende, d. h. Gott.[11]

In der einundzwanzigsten Prämisse behauptet Maimonides, dass ein Ding, das aus zwei oder mehr Teilen zusammengesetzt ist, nicht notwendig aus sich selbst existieren kann:

»Die einundzwanzigste Prämisse: Für alles aus zwei Dingen Zusammengesetzte ist jene Zusammensetzung zwingend die Ursache seiner Existenz als solches [d. h. als Zusammengesetztes]. Deshalb ist es kein aus sich selbst notwendig Existierendes, denn seine Existenz [entsteht] durch die Existenz seiner beiden Teile und ihrer Zusammensetzung.«[12]

Für Maimonides hat etwas Zusammengesetztes mehr als eine Ursache. Es benötigt sowohl seine Teile als auch deren Zusammensetzung. Etwas Zusammengesetztes kann deshalb nicht aus sich selbst heraus existieren.

Al-Tabrīzī beginnt seinen Kommentar, indem er Maimonides' Prämisse neu formuliert. Er passt nicht nur die technischen Ausdrücke an die Terminologie des 13. Jahrhunderts an, er ändert auch die Stoßrichtung von Maimonides' Prämisse:

»Der Kommentar: Jede Essenz (*māhiyya*) welche aus zwei oder mehr Teilen zusammengesetzt ist, ist zwingend aus sich selbst [entweder] möglich oder nicht existierend. Was aus sich selbst notwendig existiert ist niemals zusammengesetzt. Vielmehr ist es eines und einfach und ohne jegliche Zusammensetzung.«[13]

Schenken wir al-Tabrīzī Glauben, so behauptet die einundzwanzigste Prämisse nicht nur, dass etwas Zusammengesetztes nicht aus sich selbst heraus notwendig existieren kann. Sie behauptet vielmehr, dass etwas notwendig aus sich heraus Existierendes nicht zusammengesetzt sein kann. Es geht letztlich also darum, dass Gott, der einzig notwendig aus sich heraus Existierende, nicht zusammengesetzt ist. Die einundzwanzigste Prämisse behauptet also letztlich die Einheit Gottes.

Die so verstandene Prämisse stützt al-Tabrīzī nun mit einem demonstrativen Beweis. Seine Beweisführung ist ein klassisches Beispiel für die arabische

11 Zur Rezeption von Avicennas Essenz-Existenz Distinktion siehe Robert Wisnovsky, Essence and Existence in the Eleventh- and Twelfth-Century Islamic East (Mašriq): A Sketch, in: Dag Nikolaus Hasse (Hg.), The Arabic, Hebrew and Latin Reception of Avicenna's Metaphysics, Berlin 2011, S. 27–50.

12 Maimonides, Dalālat al-ḥā'irīn, S. 167; vgl. al-Tabrīzī, Sharḥ al-Muqaddamāt, S. 87.

13 Al-Tabrīzī, Sharḥ al-Muqaddamāt, S. 87.

Philosophie des 13. Jahrhunderts. Al-Tabrīzī sieht sich selbst in der Rolle des *muḥaqqiq*, d. h. eines Philosophen, der jede Behauptung verifiziert und argumentativ untermauert, mit dem Ziel, einen demonstrativen Beweis zu führen. Betrachten wir al-Tabrīzīs Beweis für Maimonides' einundzwanzigste Prämisse:

»Dies lässt sich so demonstrativ beweisen: [(1)] Alles [aus zwei Teilen] Zusammengesetzte bedarf zu seiner Existenz der Existenz seiner beiden Teile und [(2)] seine Teile sind etwas anderes als es [selbst]. Also [(3)] bedarf alles Zusammengesetzte zu seiner Existenz etwas anderes als sich selbst. Und [(4)] alles, das etwas anderes bedarf, wird aufgehoben durch die Aufhebung dieses anderen. Deshalb ist [(5)] alles, was durch die Aufhebung von etwas anderem aufgehoben wird, aus sich selbst möglich. Daraus ergibt sich, dass [(6)] alles Zusammengesetzte aus sich selbst möglich ist. Aber [(7)] nichts, das aus sich selbst notwendig existiert, aus sich selbst möglich ist. Daraus ergibt sich, dass [(8)] nichts Zusammengesetztes notwendig aus sich selbst existiert. Und umgekehrt ist [(9)] nichts, das notwendig aus sich selbst existiert, zusammengesetzt. Deshalb ist alles aus sich selbst notwendig Existierende absolute Einheit, bar jeglicher Verbindung und Zusammensetzung. Dies wollten wir demonstrativ beweisen.«[14]

Auf den ersten Blick verwirrt die Passage. Wenn wir uns al-Tabrīzīs Beweis aber näher betrachten, lässt sich seine Struktur leicht erkennen.
Aus den ersten beiden Prämissen …

1) Alles Zusammengesetzte bedarf zu seiner Existenz der Existenz seiner beiden Teile.
2) Die Teile eines Zusammengesetzten sind etwas anderes als das Zusammengesetzte selbst

… folgt der Satz

3) Alles Zusammengesetzte bedarf zu seiner Existenz etwas anderem als seiner selbst. [Aus (1) und (2) Jedes A ist B]

Dieser Satz ist die erste Prämisse in einem kategorischen Syllogismus (Modus »Barbara«), zu dem auch die zwei folgenden Sätze gehören:

4) Alles, was etwas anderem [als seiner selbst] bedarf, wird aufgehoben durch die Aufhebung dieses anderen. [Jedes B ist C]
5) Alles, das durch die Aufhebung von etwas anderem aufgehoben wird, ist aus sich selbst möglich. [Jedes C ist D]

14 Al-Tabrīzī, Sharḥ al-Muqaddamāt, S. 88.

Aus Sätzen (3) bis (5) folgt

6) Alles Zusammengesetzte ist aus sich selbst möglich. [Barbara aus (2)–(4) Jedes A ist D]

Dieser Satz bildet wiederum die erste Prämisse des folgenden Syllogismus (Modus »Camestres«):

7) Nichts, das aus sich selbst notwendig existiert, ist aus sich selbst möglich. [Kein E ist D]
8) Nichts Zusammengesetztes existiert notwendig aus sich selbst. [Camestres aus (6)–(7) Kein A ist E]

Die Schlussfolgerung aus diesem Syllogismus ist eigentlich Maimonides' einundzwanzigste Prämisse. Aber al-Tabrīzī konvertiert die Schlussfolgerung und erhält damit seine Interpretation von Maimonides' Prämisse:

9) Nichts, das notwendig aus sich selbst existiert, ist zusammengesetzt. [Durch einfache Konversion aus (8) Kein E ist A]

Al-Tabrīzī ist der Auffassung, dass dieser Beweis ein demonstrativer Beweis ist. Das heißt, wir stimmen den einzelnen Prämissen zwingend zu und der Beweis folgt allen Regeln der logischen Kunst.

Al-Tabrīzīs Beweis ist natürlich weder besonders komplex noch besonders originell. Aber er zeigt uns, was Maimonides' Text für einen muslimischen Philosophen des 13. Jahrhunderts attraktiv macht. Maimonides' Liste von Prämissen dient hervorragend als Skelett, das man mit Beweisen aus einer anderen philosophischen Tradition zum Leben erwecken kann. Wie schon erwähnt, benutzt al-Tabrīzī vor allem Beweise aus der Philosophie des Avicenna. Ob der so geschaffene Golem noch den Ideen des Maimonides' dient, ist natürlich eine andere Frage. Aber er verleiht der Philosophie des Avicenna Beine, die sie zurück in die jüdische Philosophie tragen.

Die Judeo-arabische und hebräische Rezeption von al-Tabrīzīs Kommentar

Tabrīzīs Kommentar wurde auch von jüdischen Philosophen gelesen, wie erhaltene arabische Handschriften in hebräischer Schrift belegen.[15] Der Kommentar wurde außerdem zweimal ins Hebräische übersetzt. Die erste Übersetzung von Isaac ben Nathan von Mallorca stammt aus dem Jahr 1347 und wurde um 1574 gedruckt; eine zweite, anonyme, Übersetzung erfuhr im Jahr 1996 eine kritische Edition.[16]

Durch die hebräische Übersetzung erhielten spätere jüdische Philosophen im Westen Zugang zu al-Tabrīzīs avicennischer Kontextualisierung von Maimonides. Bisher wissen wir von einigen hebräisch schreibenden Philosophen, die al-Tabrīzīs Kommentar gelesen haben. Unter ihnen ist der berühmte Kritiker der aristotelischen Philosophie, Chasdai Crescas (gest. 1410/11).

In den Abschnitten, die bisher untersucht wurden, scheint Crescas den von al-Tabrīzī vorgestellten Argumenten Avicennas aber nicht zu folgen. So berichtet al-Tabrīzī im Kommentar von der im Osten der islamischen Welt entwickelten Theorie des Impetus (*mayl*). Eine solche Theorie hätte Crescas bei seiner Kritik der aristotelischen Physik sehr geholfen. Er verzichtet aber auf al-Tabrīzīs Hilfe. Tzvi Langermann hat die Rezeption von al-Tabrīzīs Kommentar zu dieser Frage untersucht.[17] Er versteht sie exemplarisch als Beispiel für die unfruchtbare Weitergabe von Konzepten (*barren transmission*): Ein Text mit originellen Konzepten wird übersetzt. Und obwohl die originellen Konzepte ausgezeichnet zur Philosophie des Lesers dieser Übersetzung passen würden, ignoriert er sie komplett.

Dabei handelt es sich aber nur um eine Frage aus al-Tabrīzīs Kommentar und nur um einen Leser al-Tabrīzīs. Wir können nicht ausschließen, dass Teile der Philosophie Avicennas über al-Tabrīzīs Kommentar Einzug in die hebräische Philosophie gehalten haben.[18]

15 Siehe Gregor Schwarb, The Reception of Maimonides in Christian-Arabic Literature, S. 145.

16 Zu den hebräischen Übersetzungen siehe Moritz Steinschneider, Die hebraeischen Uebersetzungen des Mittelalters und die Juden als Dolmetscher, Berlin 1893, S. 361–363; die anonyme Übersetzung ist ediert in Maurice R. Hayoun, Moses Maimonides und Muhammad al-Tabrisi, Trumah 5 (1996), S. 201–245.

17 Y. Tzvi Langermann, No Reagent, No Reaction: The Barren Transmission of Avicennan Dynamics to Ḥasdai Crescas, Aleph, 12 (2012), S. 161–188.

18 Einen guten Überblick zum gegenwärtigen Stand der Forschung über die mittelalterliche jüdische Rezeption von Avicennas philosophischen und medizinischen Werken vermitteln Gad Freudenthal und Mauro Zonta, Avicenna Among Medieval Jews: The Reception of Avicenna's Philosophical, Scientific and Medical Writings in Jewish Cultures, East And West, Arabic Sciences and Philosophy, 22 (2012), S. 217–287.

Nicht nur wurde Maimonides' »Dalāla« also von muslimischen Philosophen gelesen. Wie der Fall von al-Tabrīzī zeigt, wurde ihre Lektüre wiederum von jüdischen Philosophen rezipiert. Mit den hier vorgestellten Philosophen ist der Kreis der muslimischen Leser von Maimonides keinesfalls erschöpft. Zukünftige Forschungen werden unser Wissen über die Maimonidesrezeption in der islamisch-arabischen Philosophie ergänzen.

Abstract
Al-Tabrīzī's Commentary to Maimonides' »The Guide for the Perplexed«: The Reception of Maimonides in Muslim-Arabic Literature

Moses Maimonides is said to have insisted that his »Guide for the Perplexed« not be transcribed from Hebrew into Arabic script. This ostensible prohibition did not keep Muslim scholars from studying Maimonides' major philosophical work. The commentary of Muḥammad ibn Abī Bakr al-Tabrīzī from the thirteenth century is an excellent example in this regard. Al-Tabrīzī discusses the list of twenty-six philosophical propositions with which Maimonides introduces in the Guide his arguments for the existence, unity, and incorporeality of God. The paper shows how al-Tabrīzī establishes the truth of Maimonides premises with the methods of 13th-century Arabic philosophy and takes a brief look at the reception of Hebrew translations of his commentary.

Lukas Muehlethaler ist Juniorprofessor für jüdische Philosophie und Ästhetik an der Freien Universität Berlin und am Zentrum Jüdische Studien Berlin-Brandenburg. Er studierte jüdische Philosophie und Geistesgeschichte an der Hebräischen Universität in Jerusalem sowie Arabistik und Islamwissenschaft an der Yale University. Dort provomierte er 2010 mit einer Arbeit über den jüdischen Philosophen Ibn Kammūna und wurde anschließend ein Mitglied der Research Unit Intellectual History of the Islamicate World an der FU-Berlin. Er forscht auf dem Gebiet der jüdischen und muslimischen Geistesgeschichte des Mittelalters und interessiert sich insbesondere für Beziehungen zwischen verschiedenen intellektuellen und kulturellen Traditionen.

Görge K. Hasselhoff

Zur Maimonidesrezeption in der christlich-lateinischen Literatur*

▸ Al-Andalus, Iberische Halbinsel ▸ Albertus Magnus ▸ aschkenasisch ▸ Buxtorf, Johannes d. J. ▸ Flavius Mithridates ▸ Giustiniani, Agostino ▸ halachisch ▸ al-Harizi, Yehuda ▸ Johannes von Capua ▸ Meister Eckhart ▸ Münster, Sebastian ▸ Nicolaus Cusanus ▸ Rabbinisch ▸ Talmud ▸ Thomas von Aquino ▸ Tibboniden, Samuel ibn Tibbon ▸ Wilhelm von Auvergne

Bekanntlich hat Moshe ben Maimon (graeco-latinisiert: Moses Maimonides) seine Werke in zwei Sprachen abgefasst, zum einen auf Arabisch, seiner Umgangs- und Muttersprache, und zum anderen – in weit geringerem Umfang – auf Hebräisch, der Sprache der rabbinischen Gelehrten. Im Zuge des Wiederaufkommens des Hebräischen als Verkehrssprache im Bereich der Iberischen Halbinsel und Südfrankreichs wurden mehrere der arabischen Schriften des Maimonides – zum Teil bereits zu seinen Lebzeiten – ins Hebräische übertragen. Diese Übersetzungstätigkeit erstreckte sich auf den Zeitraum von rund 100 Jahren; dabei kommt der Familie der Tibboniden große Bedeutung zu. Gut eine Generation nach Maimonides' Tod begann zudem eine Übersetzertätigkeit ins Lateinische, die, mit Unterbrechungen, bis ins 17. Jahrhundert andauerte.

Am Anfang steht vermutlich eine anonyme Abhandlung (»Liber de parabola« – »Buch vom Gleichnis«), der eine auszugsweise Übertragung einzelner Kapitel des III. Teils des »Führers der Unschlüssigen« eingefügt ist. Diese Übertragung ist in bislang nur einer bekannten Handschrift überliefert, scheint jedoch Wilhelm von Auvergne und Johannes von Rupella (von La Rochelle) bekannt gewesen zu sein, die ihrerseits aber nicht erkennen lassen, dass sie den Verfasser kennen.

Weiter verbreitet war eine andere Teilübersetzung, die unter dem Namen »Liber de uno deo benedicto« (»Buch von dem einen gebenedeiten Gott«) mit

* Für eine umfassende Darstellung der Thematik mit ausführlichen Bibliografien vgl. Görge K. Hasselhoff, Dicit Rabbi Moyses: Studien zum Bild von Moses Maimonides im lateinischen Westen vom 13. bis 15. Jahrhundert, Würzburg 2004; 2., erw. Aufl. 2005; sowie ders., Moses Maimonides interkulturell gelesen, Interkulturelle Bibliothek, Bd. 20, Nordhausen 2009.

Angabe des Verfassers (»Rabbi Moyses«) tradiert wurde. Bei dieser Schrift handelt es sich um eine Übertragung der 25 Sentenzen, die dem II. Buch des »Führers der Unschlüssigen« vorangestellt sind, sowie des ersten Kapitels desselben Buchs nach der Übertragung Ibn Tibbons oder der Arabischen Originalfassung. Die Schrift wurde nachweislich am Anfang der 1240er Jahre und dann noch einmal im letzten Drittel des 13. Jahrhunderts verwendet und scheint aus dem Umfeld des Pariser Dominikanerkonvents zu stammen, wie sich an Zitaten bei Moneta von Cremona und insbesondere bei Albertus Magnus ablesen lässt. Maimonides wurde durch diese Schrift als einer der arabischen Aristoteliker rezipiert, denen eine Autorität in Fragen der Ewigkeit der Welt und der Gottesbeweise zukam.

Im gleichen Umfeld entstand, aller Wahrscheinlichkeit nach als Folge der Pariser Talmuddisputation von 1240 bzw. der Talmudverbrennung von 1242/4, eine nahezu vollständige Übertragung des »Führers der Unschlüssigen« nach der Übertragung Yehuda al-Harizis. An dieser lateinischen Übertragung sticht ins Auge, dass v.a. im ersten, lexikografischen Teil des Buchs Erklärungen hebräischer Wörter ausgelassen sind. Diese Übertragung zog eine vergleichsweise breite Rezeption, insbesondere bei Autoren aus dem Predigerorden nach sich, die im 16. Jahrhundert in der Pariser Drucklegung unter der Herausgeberschaft des Bischofs von Nebbio, Corsica, Agostino Giustiniani (1470–1536), einen letzten Höhepunkt fand.

Rund dreißig Jahre nach dieser Gesamtübertragung finden sich Neuübersetzungen einzelner Kapitel aus dem »Führer der Unschlüssigen«, aber auch aus dem halachischen »Hauptwerk«, »Mischne Tora«, in den beiden polemischen Werken »Capistrum Iudeorum« (»Zaumzeug für die Juden«) und »Pugio fidei« (»Glaubensdolch«) des katalanischen Dominikanerbruders Raimundus Martini, der allem Anschein nach beide hebräischen Übertragungen, aber auch das arabische Original des »Führers der Unschlüssigen« verwendet hat. Diese Übertragungen wirkten einerseits am Anfang des 14. Jahrhunderts auf den franziskanischen Bibelkommentator Nikolaus von Lyra und andererseits im Bereich der religiösen Auseinandersetzungen auf der Iberischen Halbinsel und von dort aus weiter bis in die Kreise der christlichen Hebraistik und der christlichen Kabbala ab dem ausgehenden 15. Jahrhundert.[1]

Unabhängig von der Rezeption des Theologen und Philosophen wurden ab dem Ende des 13. Jahrhunderts ein Großteil der medizinischen Werke übersetzt, zum Teil existieren bis zu drei verschiedene Übertragungen der jeweils gleichen Schrift. Zumindest zwei Übersetzer sind namentlich bekannt: Ar-

1 Zur christlichen Kabbala vgl. Wilhelm Schmidt-Biggemann, Geschichte der christlichen Kabbala, Bd. 1: 15.–16. Jahrhundert; Bd. 2: 1600–1650; Bd. 3: 1660–1850 (Clavis Pansophiae, Bd. 10, 1–3), Stuttgart-Bad Cannstatt 2012–2013.

mengaldus Blasius und (Ps.-) Johannes von Capua[2]. Obwohl der Arzt Maimonides nicht zu den »Standardautoren« der medizinischen Fakultäten gehörte, scheint die Kenntnis seiner Schriften recht weit verbreitet gewesen zu sein. Zudem wurden sowohl sein großes »Regimen sanitatis« als auch seine große Aphorismensammlung seit dem letzten Drittel des 15. Jahrhunderts mehrfach gedruckt.

Im Vorfeld und Umkreis der entstehenden christlichen Kabbala wurden ab dem Ende des 15. Jahrhunderts weitere Übertragungen angefertigt. Insbesondere Flavius Mithridates als Übersetzer u. a. des »Briefs über die Auferstehung« sowie Sebastian Münster als Übersetzer der »Dreizehn Iqqarim bzw. Artikel« verdienen hier Erwähnung.

In der sich zeitgleich formierenden christlichen Hebraistik wurden im 16. und 17. Jahrhundert mehrere halachische Schriften übersetzt,[3] und Johannes Buxtorf d. J. fertigte schließlich im 17. Jahrhundert eine neue Übertragung des »Führers der Unschlüssigen« auf der Basis von Ibn Tibbons Übertragung an, die 1629 im Druck erschien.

Wie schon angedeutet, waren die Dominikaner anscheinend sehr interessiert an der Übertragung des »Führers der Unschlüssigen«; sie stellen im 13. und dem ersten Drittel des 14. Jahrhunderts auch die Leserschaft mit der intensivsten Maimonidesrezeption.

An erster Stelle ist hier Albertus Magnus zu nennen, der gleichsam den Weg für Maimonides in die Literatur der Scholastik öffnete. Er nennt verstreut über sein gesamtes Werk Maimonides weit über 100-mal. Insbesondere in Fragen des Gottesverständnisses und zur Frage der Ewigkeit der Welt, für die Maimonides eine Synthese von Aristotelismus und Bibelglauben angeboten hatte, wurde dem jüdischen Gelehrten vom Dominikaner hohe Autorität zuerkannt. Das ist umso bemerkenswerter, als Albertus an der Talmudverurteilung von 1248 per Unterschrift aktiv mitwirkte. In anderer Hinsicht bemerkenswert ist Thomas von Aquino, der Maimonides rund 80-mal als Autorität anführt. Moderne Autoren wie David B. Burrell haben zudem die Kongenialität von Thomas und Maimonides herauszustellen versucht, dabei jedoch ein wichtiges Detail übersehen: Noch weit häufiger als Thomas

2 Es hat den Anschein, dass der Übersetzer der maimonidischen Texte sich den Namen eines Notars lieh; vgl. dazu Görge K. Hasselhoff, Zu einigen lateinischen Fassungen des *Pañcatantra*, in: Mamoun Fansa/Eckhard Grunewald (Hg.), Von listigen Schakalen und törichten Kamelen – Die Fabel in Orient und Okzident, Schriftenreihe des Landesmuseums Natur und Mensch, 62, Wiesbaden 2008, S. 75–84, hier S. 77–80.

3 Vgl. Aaron L. Katchen/Christian Hebraists/Dutch Rabbis: Seventeenth-Century Apologetics and the Study of Maimonides' Mishneh Torah, Cambridge, Mass. u. a. 1984; Peter van Rooden, Theology, Biblical Scholarship and Rabbinical Studies in the Seventeenth Century: Constantijn L'Empereur (1591–1648), Professor of Hebrew and Theology at Leiden, Leiden u. a. 1989.

Maimonides namentlich nennt, plagiiert er ihn.[4] Darauf wurde bereits in der Mitte des 20. Jahrhunderts im Rahmen der deutschen Thomasausgabe von Hans Urs von Balthasar und Otto Maria Pesch für die Profetielehre und die Schrifthermeneutik sowie in anderem Kontext von Ernst Koplowitz und mehreren weiteren Autoren für die Gottesbeweise[5] hingewiesen. Ähnlich wie für Albertus ist auch für Thomas Maimonides wichtig in Fragen des theologischen Aristotelismus. Einen anders gearteten Zugang zu Maimonides mit einer sehr eigentümlichen eigenen Wirkungsgeschichte finden wir bei Jacobus de Voragine, dem Autor der wahrscheinlich bekanntesten Heiligenlegendensammlung überhaupt, der »Legenda aurea«: Er findet – ob einer anderen Tradition folgend, sei dahingestellt – im »Führer der Unschlüssigen« eine Berechnung des Himmelssphärenabstands, die er für die außergewöhnlich wundersame Leistung der Himmelfahrt Jesu in den Dienst stellt; diese Tradition wurde als Einzelberechnung in mehreren Handschriften gesondert tradiert.

Der zuweilen (und m. E. zu Unrecht) als »Thomist« bezeichnete[6] Meister Eckhart gehört zu den Autoren, die einen neuen Zugang zu Maimonides suchten. Für Meister Eckhart, der außergewöhnlich begabt war und Karriere sowohl im Bereich der Universität als auch innerhalb seines Ordens machte, lassen sich zwei Phasen einer Begegnung mit Maimonides ausmachen. Zunächst hatte er sehr traditionell und auf den Spuren seiner Ordensbrüder Albert, Thomas und Jacobus de Voragine Maimonides gelegentlich zitiert, scheinbar ohne ihn selbst gelesen und exzerpiert zu haben, wie sich an seinen frühen lateinischen Schriften und den ersten Fassungen seines Weisheits- und seines Exoduskommentars zeigen lässt. Wahrscheinlich im Rahmen seiner zweiten Pariser Professur (1308/9) scheint er ein Exemplar des »Dux neutrorum« selbst gelesen und exzerpiert zu haben. Insbesondere in der letzten Fassung seines Exoduskommentars sowie im »Ersten« (chronologisch wohl dem zweiten) Genesiskommentar wird Maimonides weit über 100-mal zustimmend angeführt. Neu im Vergleich zu seinen Vorgängern ist dabei u. a., dass Meister Eckhart mit Maimonides die Einheit in Gott hervorhebt – eine Aussage, die mit zur (posthumen) Verurteilung von Avignon ge-

4 Heutige katholisch-apologetische Angriffe auf diese von mir schon 2002 vorgetragene These belegen m. E. nur, dass sie nicht völlig abwegig ist.

5 Für eine Literaturübersicht vgl. Görge K. Hasselhoff, »Anmerkungen zur Rezeption des Maimonides in den Schriften des Thomas von Aquino«, in: Wolfram Kinzig/Cornelia Kück (Hg.), Judentum und Christentum zwischen Konfrontation und Faszination: Ansätze zu einer neuen Beschreibung jüdisch-christlicher Beziehungen, Stuttgart 2002, S. 55–73, hier S. 63, Anm. 29.

6 Vgl. z. B. jüngst Jean Devriendt, »Der Intellekt in den lateinischen Predigten Meister Eckharts«, in: Harald Schwaetzer/Marie-Anne Vannier (Hg.), Zum Intellektverständnis bei Meister Eckhart und Nikolaus von Kues, Münster 2012, S. 49–63, hier S. 62.

führt hat. Womöglich hängt hiermit auch zusammen, dass die Schriften des Maimonides in den nachfolgenden rund 100 Jahren von christlichen Autoren kaum noch angerührt wurden, geschweige denn ihr Verfasser namentlich genannt wurde. Erst durch Dionysius den Kartäuser und dessen Freund Nicolaus Cusanus wurde Maimonides wieder als ernstzunehmender Autor wahrgenommen, der in der aufkommenden Hebraistik eine Renaissance erfuhr.

Überblickt man die hier ausgebreitete Spanne von knapp dreihundert Jahren, so lassen sich verschiedene Wellen einer christlichen Maimonidesrezeption erkennen. Sollte die anonyme Teilübertragung des »Liber de Parabola« tatsächlich aus den 1230er Jahren stammen, so zeigt das, dass mit ihr noch ein vergleichsweise traditioneller jüdischer Text, der in der Tradition des im Westen neu bekannt werdenden Talmud sowie der aschkenasischen Talmud- und Bibelkommentare stand, Eingang in christliches Denken fand. Mit der Anklage des Talmud durch Nikolaus Donin wandelte sich das christlich-jüdische Verhältnis jedoch fundamental. Im Umkreis des Dominikanerordens, der einen großen Anteil an der antitalmudischen und damit antijudaistischen Stimmung der Zeit hatte, wurde gleichzeitig der Aristoteliker Maimonides entdeckt, der zu einem nicht-talmudischen und damit als positiv erachteten, jüdisch-rationalistischen Gegentypus stilisiert wurde. Entsprechend wurde Maimonides in der Mitte des 13. Jahrhunderts wahrgenommen und zumeist unter Nennung seines Namens rezipiert. Dass er dabei nicht auf den Aristotelismus beschränkt wahrgenommen wurde, zeigen Hinweise auf seine Religionszugehörigkeit z. B. bei Albertus Magnus. Für Thomas von Aquino wurde gerade das aber auch zu einem Problem, weswegen er Maimonides teilweise plagiierte. Liest man dagegen nur die Textstellen, an denen Maimonides namentlich angeführt wird, so entsteht über weite Strecken ein Bild von einem nicht-rationalen und nicht-aristotelischen Juden. Ein vergleichbarer Umgang mit der Nicht-Nennung der Quelle findet sich beispielsweise auch beim dem Franziskanischen Ordensgeneral Matthäus von Aquasparta.

Um die Wende zum 14. Jahrhundert differenzierte sich die christliche Sichtweise auf Maimonides in mehrfacher Hinsicht: Zum einen verbreiterte sich die Grundlage an Schriften von Maimonides, die gelesen werden konnten: Sowohl vereinzelte halachische Texte als auch medizinische Abhandlungen wurden neu übersetzt; zudem lasen Autoren wie Meister Eckhart oder Heinrich Batenus von Mechelen Maimonides gründlich von neuem und ließen ihre Kenntnis in ihre eigenen Werke einfließen. Nun wurde auch der Neuplatoniker Maimonides schärfer konturiert. Ab den 1330er Jahren jedoch bricht die theologisch-philosophische Maimonideslektüre vorerst ab, wohl auch, weil sich das theologische Interesse verschoben hatte.

Im 15. Jahrhundert lässt sich einerseits eine Art Maimonidesrenaissance bei Autoren wie Dionysius dem Kartäuser feststellen, andererseits kommen seit der Frühhebraistik auch die hebräischen bzw. hebräisch übersetzten Quellen neu in den Blick. Einen vorläufigen Abschluss stellt die Edition der mittelalterlichen Übertragung des »Dux neutrorum« im Rahmen des neuplatonischen Editionsprogramms des Orientalisten Agostino Giustinani OP dar, mit dem einerseits eine mittelalterliche Tradition kanonisiert und – durch die Schriftform – gewissermaßen vulgarisiert wurde, und andererseits *eine* Grundlage für die aufkommende Christliche Kabbala gelegt wurde.

Abstract
Meister Eckhart reads Maimonides: On the Reception of Maimonides in Christian-Latin Literature

The article provides an overview over the medieval Latin translations of Maimonides' œuvre. The driving force of its translations seems to have been the Dominican Order. Most of the readers of the philosophical and theological works were Dominicans such as Thomas Aquinas and Meister Eckhart.

At the turn of the 14th century also medical works were translated.

Görge K. Hasselhoff studierte Evangelische Theologie, Philosophie und Jüdische Studien in Bielefeld, Marburg, Heidelberg und Berlin. 2008-2014 war er Research Scholar im Käte Hamburger Kolleg »Dynamiken der Religionsgeschichte zwischen Asien und Europa« an der Ruhr-Universität Bochum mit einem Projekt zu der »Bedeutung des Bibel- und Talmudkommentars Rabbi Shlomo Yitzhaqi (Raschi) für das lateinische Christentum«.

Schwerpunkte seiner Arbeit sind Kirchengeschichte, die Geschichte der christlich-jüdischen Beziehungen in Antike und Mittelalter sowie Hermann Cohen und die Wissenschaft des Judentums.

Yitzhak Y. Melamed

"Let the Law Cut through the Mountain": Salomon Maimon, Moses Mendelssohn, and Mme. Truth

▸ Haskalah (Maskilim) ▸ Rabbi Dov Ber of Mezerich ▸ Rabbinic ▸ Wolffians ▸ Zohar

> "Eternal truths have nothing to do with the majority of votes, and least of all where the truth is of such a nature that it leaves all expression behind."[1]

Introduction

Moses Maimonides was a rare kind of radical. Being a genuine Aristotelian, he recommended following the middle path and avoiding extremism. Yet, within the sphere of Jewish philosophy and thought, he created a school of philosophical radicalism, inspiring rabbis and thinkers to be unwilling to compromise their integrity in searching for the truth, regardless of where their arguments might lead. Both Spinoza and Salomon Maimon inherited this commitment to uncompromising philosophical inquiry. But of course, such willingness to follow a philosophical argument to any length is a fine prescription for getting into trouble with both community and political leaders. In this paper I trace the story of one such collision that took place between the radical philosopher Salomon Maimon and the bourgeois Enlightenment politician, Moses Mendelssohn.

Maimonidean Radicalism

In order to grasp the scale of the scandal of Maimonides' philosophical radicalism, let me quote from a letter by Rabbi Jacob Emden (1697–1776), written more than five centuries after Maimonides' death. This rather late perspec-

1 Solomon Maimon, An Autobiography, trans. J. Clark Murray with an introduction by Michael Shapiro, Urbana and Chicago, University of Illinois Press 2001, p. 232.

tive can help us to understand Maimonides' reputation in mainstream Rabbinic thought:

"I do not deny speaking critically of the 'Guide of the Perplexed' — which I believe was never composed by Maimonides, the one who wrote the 'Code' [*Yad ha-Hazaka*] whom we pride ourselves in (or perhaps there were two Maimonides? Yet, even the 'Book of Science' contains some of the mistaken opinions of the 'Guide of the Perplexed') ... I cannot conceive how such a misshape could come out of the hands of this great Jewish man, great in Torah and deeds, as the famous Rabbi Moses...and though there is in the book some piety, some support for faith and remedy against anthropomorphism, and this may save the entire book, yet the honey is sunk in much poison and the remedy in the destructive vanity of philosophy."[2]

Emden was no fanatic. Many scholars consider him the precursor of the Haskalah.[3] His autobiography, "Megillat Sefer", is quite a bold and daring text, and he rarely shied away from challenging traditional opinions, such as the antiquity of the "Zohar", the canonical text of the Kabbalah. Indeed, Moses Mendelssohn, the godfather of the Jewish Enlightenment movement, referred to Emden as his own rabbinic authority.[4] Against this context, one can appreciate Emden's astonishment and embarrassment at the radical claims of Maimonides' "Guide" and "Book of Science"; an astonishment that made him suggest that perhaps there were two writers named "Maimonides."

I will not dwell here on the critical reception of Maimonides' philosophical radicalism or the series of "Maimonidean controversies" that dominated the late Jewish Middle Ages.[5] I do wish, however, to unfold the story of one modern transformation of such a controversy, a controversy that arose not over any particular claim of Maimonides, but rather over one person's intellectual duty to examine philosophical arguments according to their validity and soundness, not the political and religious reputation of their author. Speaking of the author in question, Benedict de Spinoza (1632–1677), let me suggest that Spinoza himself belonged to the "great chain" of Maimonidean radicals, not because he adhered to Maimonides' philosophy (Spinoza was highly

2 Rabbi Jacob Emden, *Iggeret Purim*, 30v in: Jacob J. Schacter, Rabbi Jacob Emden's *Iggeret Purim*, in: Isadore Twersky (ed.), Studies in Medieval Jewish History and Literature, Cambridge, Harvard University Press 1984, vol. 2, p. 445. The translation from the Hebrew is mine.

3 See, for example, David Sorkin, Moses Mendelssohn and the Religious Enlightenment, Berkeley and Los Angeles, University of California Press 1996, p. 157.

4 See Alexander Altmann, Moses Mendelssohn: A Biographical Study, Philadelphia, Jewish Publication Society of America 1973, pp. 217–218.

5 For a helpful survey of the Maimonidean controversies, see Haim Hillel Ben Sasson/Raphael Jospe/Dov Schwartz, Maimonidean Controversy, in: Encyclopedia Judaica, 2nd ed., Detroit, Thomson Gale 2007, vol. 13, pp. 371–381.

critical of many of Maimonides' claims), but rather because he adopted the same iconoclastic attitude that motivated Maimonides' battle against anthropomorphism and idolatry.[6] Spinoza frequently refers to Maimonides, both explicitly and implicitly. Since one of the main features of Spinoza's writing is its polemic nature, it will come as no surprise that these references are almost always critical. Indeed, Spinoza rarely refers to authors with whom he agrees. But his recurrent responses and allusions to Maimonides make it clear that Maimonides was a significant interlocutor in his thought. In terms of philosophical positions, Spinoza considered himself a critic of Aristotelianism.[7] Indeed, in one of the very rare moments in which he bestows praise on a predecessor, he commends Rabbi Hisdai Crescas, an anti-Aristotelian and anti-Maimonidean of the late 14th century, for his unequivocal rejection of the Aristotelian ban on actual infinity.[8]

The Knight from Suchowyborg and Lady T.

Salomon Maimon's life story is as fascinating as it is hard to believe. Growing up in traditional Jewish surroundings in Lithuania, Maimon developed a deep interest in medieval Jewish philosophy in his early teens, and Maimonides' "Guide of the Perplexed" had an enduring influence on him. Maimon's attachment to Maimonides — both personally and philosophically — ran throughout his life.[9] Even Maimon's own name was adopted as an expression of respect for this teacher (Before taking the surname 'Maimon', he was called after his father: *Shlomo* [Salomon] *ben* ("son of") *Joshua*). The uncompromising and iconoclastic spirit of medieval Maimonideanism struck a deep chord in his psyche and launched him on an obsessive, life-long search after the truth. Upon hearing about the supposed appearance of "Lady Truth" in the

6 For an excellent discussion of the Maimonidean elements in Spinoza's thought, see Warren Zev Harvey, Portrait of Spinoza as Maimonidean, in: Journal of the History of Philosophy, 20 (1981), pp. 151–172. For Spinoza's critique of anthropomorphism and anthropocentrism, see my "Spinoza's Anti-Humanism: An Outline", in: Carlos Fraenkel, Dario Perinetti, Justin Smith (eds.), The Rationalists, Kluwer – New Synthese Historical Library 2010, pp. 147–166.

7 See Spinoza's preface to the "Theological Political Treatise" (Geb. III/9), as well as Chapter Thirteen (Geb. III/168).

8 Spinoza, Ep.12 (Geb. IV/62/1).

9 Maimon dedicated ten (!) chapters of his autobiography to an elucidation of Maimonides' "Guide" (see Zwi Batscha (ed.), Salomon Maimons Lebensgeschichte, Frankfurt a. M., Jüdischer Verlag 1995, pp. 240–315. These chapters are omitted in the existing English translation.)

emerging Hassidic movement, Maimon rushed to the court of the leader of the movement, the *Maggid* of Mezerich (Rabbi Dov Ber of Mezerich, 1710(?)–1772),[10] but was disappointed to find out that the Lady had just left the place (or at least so the rumor said). Then came the idea that perhaps Berlin, the city of the *Aufklärer*, was the Lady's new place of residence (alas, had he only known …), and in 1777 Maimon packed a small bag of food and some manuscripts (including an early commentary on the "Guide"), said goodbye to his wife and young children and departed for Berlin. He then began an odyssey of 10 or 12 years, in which he succeeded, among other things, in being kicked out of the shelter of the Jewish community in Berlin due to his engagement with Maimonides' "Guide",[11] learning and pursuing the delicate art of beggary,[12] returning to Berlin and becoming a protégé of Mendelssohn,[13] getting into a quarrel with Mendelssohn (on account of Maimon's unhidden Spinozism, and his frequent visits to certain not-so-respected houses, as we shall shortly see), leaving Berlin to go to Amsterdam (for it was said that Lady T. was fond of a certain local Benedict),[14] being stoned in the open street by the children of the Jewish community in Amsterdm, attending a Gymnasium at Altona at the age of 30,[15] and finally landing back in Berlin shortly after Mendelssohn's death. Then, the Lady was glimpsed again between the lines of Kant's "Critique of Pure Reason".[16] Well, this story is only beginning, and I invite you to consult other books — such as Maimon's own "Lebensgeschichte" (1792/3) — if you wish to find out the end of this obsessive affair. Let me just warn you not to expect a happy ending. I turn now to examine Maimon's encounter with Moses Mendelssohn more closely.

Maimon, Mendelssohn, and Spinoza's Specter

Maimon's second visit to Berlin, between 1780 and 1783, seems to have been a success story. During this visit he made the important acquaintance of Mendelssohn and succeeded in making his way into some circles of the Jewish Enlightenment. It was probably in this period that Maimon first came across Spinoza's writings. In his autobiography, Maimon describes this discovery:

10 Maimon, Autobiography, pp. 151–175.
11 Ibid, pp. 193–196.
12 Ibid, pp. 197–199.
13 Ibid, pp. 210–216.
14 Ibid, pp. 245–252.
15 Ibid, pp. 258–264.
16 Ibid, pp. 279–283.

"As a man altogether without experience I carried my frankness at times a little too far and brought upon myself many vexations in consequence. I was reading Spinoza. His profound thought and his love of truth pleased me uncommonly; and as his system had already been suggested to me in Poland by the Kabbalistic writings, I began to reflect upon it anew and became so convinced of its truth, that all the efforts of Mendelssohn to change my opinion were unavailing. I answered all the objections brought against it by the Wolffians, raised objections against their system myself, and showed that if the *Definitiones nominales* of the Wolffian ontology are converted into *Definitiones reales*, conclusions of the very opposite of theirs are the result.[17] *Moreover, I could not explain the persistency of Mendelssohn and the Wolffians generally in adhering to their system, except as a political dodge and a piece of hypocrisy* [*politische Kniffe und Heuchelei*], by which they studiously endeavored to descend to the mode of thinking common in the popular mind; and this conviction I expressed openly and without reserve."[18]

It is worth noting that Mendelssohn himself expressed deep appreciation for Spinoza in his early "Philosophische Gespräche" (1755). In this work Mendelssohn attempted to domesticate Spinoza's radicalism and suggested that Spinoza's philosophy was not that different from Leibniz's orthodox view, although he held that Spinoza had gone somewhat astray. Thus, claimed Mendelssohn, we should appreciate Spinoza as having cleared the way for the appearance of Leibniz.[19] It is not hard to tell what Mendelssohn's sincere view of the relationship between the philosophies of Spinoza and Leibniz was. Mendelssohn praised Leibniz for being "not merely the greatest, but also the most careful [*behutsamste*] philosopher."[20]

"If Leibniz had openly confessed he borrowed the essential part of his harmony from Spinoza, tell me, would these people not have believed from the outset that they found in the reference to Spinoza's name the basis for refuting this doctrine? Quite certainly."[21]

17 Kant seems to make a similar point in his lectures on metaphysics: "If I derive the existence [*Dasein*] of the *ens realissimum* from its concept, this is the path to Spinozism" (AA 28:786). Cf. my "'*Omnis determinatio est negatio*' – Determination, Negation and Self-Negation in Spinoza, Kant, and Hegel," in: Eckart Förster, Yitzhak Y. Melamed (eds.), Spinoza and German Idealism, Cambridge, Cambridge University Press 2012, pp. 182–183.

18 Maimon, Autobiography, pp. 219–220 = Lebensgeschichte, pp. 156–57. Italics added.

19 "Before the transition from the Cartesian to the Leibnizian philosophy could occur, it was necessary for someone to take the plunge into the monstrous abyss lying between them. This unhappy lot fell to Spinoza. How his fate is to be pitied! He was a sacrifice for the human intellect." (Moses Mendelssohn, Philosophical Writings, ed. Daniel O. Dahlstrom, Cambridge, Cambridge University Press 1997, p. 106).

20 Mendelssohn, Philosophical Writings, 104 = Gesammelte Schriften: Jubiläumsausgabe, Stuttgart/Bad Cannstatt, Frommann Verlag 1971, vol. I, p. 12.

21 Ibid.

Maimon's openness in these matters brought him trouble rather than appreciation. In his "Lebensgeschichte" Maimon tells us about the response of his fellow young Jewish *Aufklärer*:

> "My friends and well-wishers, who for the most part had never themselves speculated on philosophical subjects, but blindly adopted the results of the systems prevailing at the time as if they were established truth, did not understand me, and therefore also were unable to follow me in my opinions."[22]

The young, liberal, *maskilim* with whom Maimon used to pass time in Berlin complained to Mendelssohn that Maimon was spreading "dangerous opinions and systems" (referring ostensibly to Maimon's Spinozism).[23] Mendelssohn summoned Maimon and asked him about this and other rumors he had heard about Maimon's all-too-free behavior.[24] Maimon responded to the "charge" of Spinozism by insisting that,

> "[t]he opinion and systems referred to are either true or false. *If the former, then I do not see how the knowledge of the truth can do any harm. If the latter, then let them be refuted.* Moreover, I have explained these opinions and systems only to gentlemen who desire to be enlightened, and to rise above all prejudices."[25]

Understanding that his presence in Berlin had become a burden, Maimon bade Mendelssohn farewell, and left the city.[26]

Maimon was not expelled from Berlin by an edict of a dark fanatic rabbi, but rather through the endeavors of his liberal, enlightened friends, and with the quiet support of the Enlightement's saint and paragon of tolerance, Moses Mendelssohn. The real importance of this story lies in what it tells us about the nature of the Berlin Haskalah, its notion of tolerance, and its intellectual qualities.

Epilogue

Both Spinoza and Maimon owed a great debt to the author of the "Guide of the Perplexed". For both, the experience of reading the book seems to have played a formative role, though both grew and developed into genuine and in-

22 Maimon, Autobiography, p. 220 = Lebensgeschichte, p. 157.
23 Ibid, p. 240 = Lebensgeschichte, p. 172.
24 Ibid, pp. 238–240 = Lebensgeschichte, pp. 171–172.
25 Ibid, p. 240 = Lebensgeschichte, p. 172. Italics added.
26 For a detailed study of Maimon's engagement with Spinoza, see my "Salomon Maimon and the Rise of Spinozism in German Idealism", in: Journal of the History of Philosophy 42, January 2004, pp. 67–96.

dependent philosophers. While the mature Spinoza and Maimon could not be described as Maimonideans, insofar as they did not strictly adhere to his doctrines, they do render much of the iconoclastic spirit of their old master. More than anything else, they affirmed uncompromising commitment to pursue philosophical arguments regardless of where they might lead. This kind of commitment is precisely what the mediocrity of the liberal bourgeoisie — in 18th-century Jewish Berlin, or anywhere else — could never swallow.

Abstract
Maimon, Mendelssohn und Mme. Truth

Maimonides war ein Radikaler von seltener Art. Als überzeugter Aristoteliker empfahl er den Weg der Mitte und die Vermeidung von Extremen. In der jüdischen Philosophie jedoch begründete er eine Schule des radikalen Denkens, die bei der Suche nach Wahrheit keinerlei Kompromisse zulässt, egal, wohin sie einen führt. Sowohl Spinoza als auch Salomon Maimon übernahmen diese Selbstverpflichtung zur unnachgiebigen philosophischen Erkundung. In meinem Artikel zeichne ich die Geschichte der Kollision zwischen dem radikalen Philosophen Salomon Maimon und dem bürgerlichen Aufklärungspolitiker Moses Mendelssohn nach.

Yitzhak Y. Melamed is a professor in the Department of Philosophy at Johns Hopkins University. He holds an M. A. in philosophy and the history of science and logic from Tel Aviv University, and a Ph.D. in philosophy from Yale University (2005). He has been awarded the Fulbright, Mellon, and American Academy for Jewish Research Fellowships. Recently, he also won the ACLS Burkhardt (2011), NEH (2010), and Humboldt (2011) fellowships for his forthcoming book on Spinoza and German Idealism.

George Y. Kohler

Maimonides and the Moderns

▸ Haskalah (Maskilim) ▸ Mishnah ▸ Ostjudentum ▸ Rabbinic ▸ Reformjudentum ▸ Rosenzweig, Franz ▸ Talmud ▸ Wellhausen, Julius ▸ Wissenschaft des Judentums ▸ Windelband, Wilhelm, and Rickert, Heinrich

In April 1918, shortly after the Jewish holy day of Pessah, a funeral procession took to the streets of Berlin. On its way to Berlin-Weissensee, the location of the largest Jewish cemetery in Europe, most of the people who followed the deceased were so-called *Ostjuden*—at least if we believe the account of the event given by Franz Rosenzweig—and only very few of the closest friends and colleagues of the deceased led the procession. On April 4th 1918, Professor Hermann Cohen had passed away, the first Jewish *ordinarius* in the humanities at a Prussian university and at the same time probably the most important philosopher of Judaism at the beginning of the 20th century. In his necrology, one of Cohen's most faithful disciples, Benzion Kellermann, a rabbi and philosopher in his own right (unfortunately largely forgotten today), made a most impressive claim: Maimonides, said Kellermann, stood for Cohen even above Kant.[1] To fully appreciate the weight of this sentence it is necessary to recall that Cohen is known and celebrated for his decisive contribution to neo-Kantian philosophy—of all things. After leaving the Breslau Rabbinical Seminary, Cohen studied philosophy in Berlin and devoted the first three of his many books to the interpretation of Immanuel Kant's critical system. Neo-Kantianism at this time was the ruling trend of German *Katheder-philosophie* and would soon become concentrated in two major centers: a Baden school around Wilhelm Windelband and Heinrich Rickert, and a Marburg school with Hermann Cohen as its main representative.

On the other hand, we have this medieval Jewish scholastic later called Maimonides, writing Aristotelian philosophy in Arabic, admittedly for an elitist audience, with his metaphysics based on the science of his day and his reading of the Bible still far from any critical approach. Why would this Maimonides then be still more important than Kant himself to a neo-Kantian

1 Benzion Kellermann, Die religionsphilosophische Bedeutung Hermann Cohens, in: Neue Jüdische Monatshefte, 1917/1918, p. 372: "… in gewisser Hinsicht steht ihm Maimonides noch höher als Kant …"

German idealist with some Jewish roots? And to be sure, Hermann Cohen was not interested in Maimonides for historical or sentimental reasons; the history of philosophy, Cohen explains, is always "afflicted by the independent interest of speculation".[2] Therefore, if Kellermann was right with his claim (and I think he was), Hermann Cohen must have discovered in Maimonidean thought something that did not merely correspond closely to central aspects of his own idealist philosophy. He would probably even consider Maimonides one of the major sources of this special kind of religious rationalism that was to guarantee a better, more moral future for the whole of humanity.[3]

It is only at the turn of the 20th century, a few years before retiring from his chair in Marburg, that Hermann Cohen re-read Maimonides' major philosophical work, the "Guide of the Perplexed", and increasingly based his own religious thought on the radical ideas of his medieval predecessor. In 1908 Cohen published a controversial book-length essay on what he perceived as Maimonides' ethics-centered interpretation of Judaism, an interpretation that largely corresponded with Cohen's own. And in his highly influential posthumous work "Religion of Reason out of the Sources of Judaism" (1918), the major trends of Maimonides' writing are almost identical for Cohen with those sources and a rational concept of Judaism. But, as it is true for many other aspects of Cohen's sophisticated Jewish theology found in his last book, his extensive use of Maimonidean theories for a liberal and rational interpretation of Judaism is only the climax of a long development beginning early in the 19th century with the thought of the first Jewish Reform theologians whose legacy was very important to Cohen.

In general, three sometimes overlapping phases can be distinguished in the rediscovery of Maimonides' religious philosophy in modern Germany: the first period stretches from 1742, from the first modern printing of Maimonides' "Guide", until roughly 100 years later, when the Jewish Reformers began to instrumentalise Maimonides more intensively for an agenda of religious change. The first century of a modern reception of Maimonides' theology was primarily marked by the many different attempts to provide accessible and reliable editions of the "Guide", both in Hebrew and in German translation, the languages used by potential readers. It was in those years that not only the *maskilim,* but also most of the later influential Reform rabbis and *Wissenschaft des Judentums* scholars studied the "Guide" for the first time. When Maimonidean thought was utilized in this period for proposing modernising ideas, it was above all Maimonides' openness towards secular studies

2 Hermann Cohen, Charakteristik der Ethik Maimunis, in: Hermann Cohen, Werke, Bd. 15, ed. Hartwig Wiedebach, Hildesheim 2009, p. 219 (German: "Gefahr eines selbstständigen Interesses der Spekulation.")

3 On these topics, see my book, Reading Maimonides' Philosophy in 19th Century Germany, Dordrecht, Springer 2012.

and his apparent independence from Talmudic exegesis that impressed Jewish thinkers. Only in a second period, reaching into the 1870s, did many Reform theologians discover in certain doctrines of the medieval work a mighty potential for the justification and grounding of religious reforms. Here, it was especially Maimonides' original and teleological Biblical interpretations and his rational, historicising understanding of the reasons for the commandments which often provided the Reformers with the welcome support of an accepted rabbinic authority. But only in the last phase of the modern rediscovery of the "Guide", ending with the First World War, did Maimonides' *philosophical* contribution to Jewish theology come to be fully appreciated. It is now that an essential shift of focus takes place, from the legal aspects of Judaism, not only to metaphysics, but primarily to ethics, in the study of Maimonides. With the establishment of religious philosophy as an independent and prolific discipline within the *Wissenschaft des Judentums*, the "Guide" was now read as a valuable document confirming the newly established theory that the Judaism of the Biblical prophets was a universal and humanistic religion of reason, with ethics as its main component. Maimonides' radical concept of God, philosophically expressed in his teaching about the divine attributes, became a main contribution to the development of what would be called the theology of *ethical monotheism.*

It is here that Hermann Cohen's reading of Maimonides begins – a reading that may serve us as the prime example of a modernist approach to the medieval philosopher's thinking. There are three major fields in which Cohen described Maimonides as his most influential Jewish source for the construction of a systematic theology for a *religion of reason*:

a) in the development of a philosophical concept of God that is "more" than a Kantian *postulate* but still "less" than a *persona*;
b) in the transformation of the traditional Jewish concept of a personal redeemer, the Messiah, into what can be called universal 'religious socialism';
c) in the discussion of a continued authority of Mosaic law for a modernized Judaism that is now essentially conceived of as ethical monotheism.

Whether Cohen here uses Maimonidean thought to explain his own philosophy, or vice versa he uses his own systematic logic to explain how Maimonides works, at least from 1908 onwards we find ample proof that Cohen's thinking is developing in a constant dialog with the "Guide" and some of Maimonides' other works. First and foremost, it is a rational concept of *God as Creator* that Cohen wants to derive from the "Guide" as the basis for a modern, liberal and ethical theology. Cohen does not hide the fact that he is applying his own methodology to Maimonides' teachings in order to arrive at the desired results; it even seems that he believes that only with the support of this method can Maimonides' true intentions be expressed and established. By associating Maimonidean theories with the logical concept of *infinite judgment,* Cohen is able to construct a concept of God that is highly compatible with the traditional Jewish God of *Bereshit*, the Creator of the universe. The price to be paid to tradition is nevertheless twofold. First, the resulting mode of creation is ongoing and not to be reduced to a certain point in time. While this idea of a continuously creating God is not new to Jewish thinking (and liturgy), the other concession that Cohen needs to make to traditional concepts is more painful: This Cohenean creator-God obviously needs man in the same way man needs God. God is an Idea.

Interestingly, when Maimonides praises 'intellectual perfection' in the "Guide" as the highest human perfection, this is interpreted by Cohen as an *ethical* concept. Thus, the question arises as to how this ethical perfection is supposed to be actualised in history, in other words, how this world can in fact become a better place. For an answer to this question, Cohen instrumentalized another prominent idea of Jewish tradition, the concept of messianism. Cohen believes that the idea of a unified ethical humanity, realized in the messianic future, is clearly pronounced by the Biblical prophets. Frequently Cohen calls his own version of the messianic idea *prophetic messianism*, thus emphasizing its source in that part of Scripture that Jewish Reform theology had long favored over the 'legalistic' Pentateuch. Their strict monotheism, their social concern, their rejection of meaningless ritual and their desire for universal peace made the Hebrew Prophets the ideal Scriptural reference for the Reform theologians. When later Protestant Biblical criticism dated the ancient prophets even before the legal corpus of the Pentateuch, some liberal Jewish thinkers, Cohen included, felt tempted to confirm the superiority of the prophetic books, although they knew that Julius Wellhausen in particular used this theory to claim superiority for a Christianity that stands in the moral tradition of the Hebrew prophets over a Judaism that followed Pharisaic legalism.

But *prophetic messianism*, and to the same extent what the Talmudic rabbis later read into the messianic message of the Biblical prophets, posed two serious difficulties for a straight integration into Cohen's own philosophical vision of an ideal future. For one thing, both prophetic and Talmudic Messianism are still permeated by mythology. One has to think only of the myth of the *Golden Age,* which is so prevalent in Isaiah. For another thing, it is important for Cohen to reject every form of eudaemonism in the literary sources of his Messianism: The *imitatio dei* must be a moral enterprise only and not aim at any kind of *material paradise*, the way the Talmud often pictures the messianic era. In both cases Maimonides is again of great use to Cohen. Drawing on Maimonides' commentary on the Mishnah and the "Laws of Repentance" in his "Mishneh Torah", Cohen is able to show that both texts not only disqualify selfishness as the aim of a purposeful life, replacing it with Torah study, but that they even go as far as to explicitly demythologise the Messianic age. Maimonides' Messiah is a mortal, worldly king whose task it is to rebuild a sovereign Jewish state as the precondition for the renewed fulfillment of all Biblical commandments. Thus cleansed of all objectionable elements with the help of Maimonides, Cohen can proceed to the most important part of his messianic theory. He takes up the Maimonidean thought that messianism is first and foremost distinguished by an increase of human knowledge, specifically the knowledge of God. For Maimonides, freedom from all worldly distress facilitates intensive learning in the messianic age, as 'intellectual perfection' has no empirical obstacle anymore. As we saw, for Cohen this translates directly into the acknowledgement of ethical values. To define the central characteristic of messianism, Cohen now applies Maimonides' principle of human self-perfection, which figures so prominently in the final chapters of the "Guide". Cohen reads Maimonides as replacing the traditional waiting for the mythical hereafter with man's pursuit of self-perfection, that is, the approximation of (*Annäherung an*) God. Messianism thus becomes an active, future-oriented concept in which the individual's drive for ethical perfection brings about the ideal society for all humanity.

This concept contains an element that Cohen saw as new and even revolutionary: It specifically directed Judaism's outlook toward the future. Being stuck in a debate about its past traditions, Jewish theology hardly contributes to the ethical perfection of humanity, Cohen argues. The justification of a continued existence of Judaism must be derived from the future, not from the past, because, in Cohen's eyes, the authority of the past seems to be abolished by modernity. Jewish messianism — in the form Maimonides gave it by associating it with the active increase of the human intellectual capacity — becomes Cohen's version of an ideal society. Maimonides, Cohen writes emphatically, has marked messianism "with the main features of ethical socialism".[4]

This turn to the future as the ethical criterion of Judaism also determines Cohen's position concerning the authority of Mosaic Law within the Jewish religion. Based on Maimonides' discussion of the reasons for the Biblical commandments in the third part of the "Guide of the Perplexed", and especially on what Cohen conceives of as Maimonides' strict division between Torah on the one hand and wisdom on the other, he categorically rationalised the concept of Jewish law. Disconnecting law historically from the revelation at Mount Sinai, as well as from the theological dogma of the divine lawgiver, Cohen integrates Torah law into his own philosophical concept of jurisprudence as the guarantor of human morality. Using as example Maimonides' controversial discussion of animal sacrifice in the service of God, Cohen ar-

4 Hermann Cohen, Religion der Vernunft aus den Quellen des Judentums, Frankfurt 1929, p. 361: "…die Grundzüge des ethischen Sozialismus in ihm verzeichnet und festgelegt."

rives at the conclusion that pure monotheism must ultimately be based on legal regulations for the entire society—and not on single instructions given by God to individual humans. Cohen is interested in Maimonides' rationalist theory of the law as a defense against idolatry, seen by him as preserving Judaism's monotheistic essence for the future project of messianism. Thus, the new criterion for the decision about the outdatedness of certain commandments is their contribution to this preservation of monotheism as the condition for human culture in general.

What generally interests Cohen about Maimonides' thought is the "Guide's" proposal of 'Jewish universalism', on the one hand, while on the other hand maintaining a strong stance against mythology, and against poly- and pantheism. As such, the "Guide" becomes a valuable comrade-in-arms for Cohen's lifelong struggle against mysticism, which is for him antithetically opposed to philosophy and thus responsible for all intellectual evil. What makes Maimonides attractive for Cohen is that his philosophy, in contrast to that of other medieval Jewish thinkers, does not seem to contain any nationalistic stratum: Neither the holiness of land nor of the Jewish people is important for Maimonides, but only rational truth as such—independent of its messenger. Maimonides' exclusive pursuit of philosophical truth, for which he declares himself to be ready to sacrifice all religious dogma, is an ideal point of reference for Cohen, especially because Maimonides clearly seems to agree with Cohen that this truth can be derived from the literary sources of Judaism. Cohen's own project, to provide a philosophical basis for the missionary ambitions of a modernized Jewish religion, based on the theory that only Judaism is able to lay the groundwork for a universal religion of reason—this project finds vital support in Maimonides.

Thus, Hermann Cohen is not only a typical representative of the dramatic rediscovery of Maimonides' religious philosophy in 19th-century Germany; he might well be considered the very climax of this development. Astonishingly, over a little more than 100 years Jewish thinkers re-vitalised large parts of a medieval treatise on the philosophy of religion and put them in the direct service of a radical modernization of religious thought and practice. That such a surprising enterprise was possible attests to the eternal greatness of Maimonides himself as well as to the urgent need of the rational modern age for a way of religious expression centered on a universal ethics.

Abstract
Die deutsch-jüdische Entscheidung für Maimonides als Galionsfigur einer jüdisch-universalistischen Ethik

Am Beispiel Hermann Cohens, des bedeutendsten jüdischen Philosophen um die Wende zum 20. Jahrhundert, zeigt dieser Artikel, wie moderne jüdische Denker die Maimonidische Philosophie wiederentdeckten und neu auslegten im Sinne ihrer eigenen Programme für religiöse Reformen und für die Formulierung einer liberalen jüdischen Theologie. Maimonides' radikal negativer Gottesbegriff, sein diesseitiger Messianismus und vor allem sein rationaler Umgang mit dem Zeremonialgesetz galten als ideale Ausgangspunkte für das ehrgeizige Projekt, eine modernisierte jüdische Religion weiterhin in den mittelalterlichen Denktraditionen des Judentums zu verankern.

George Y. Kohler was born in 1966 in Leipzig and grew up in East Berlin. After 1989 he worked as a radio journalist and book author. He immigrated to Israel in 1998, where he discovered the philosophy of Judaism. In 2010 he finished a dissertation on the reception of Maimonides' philosophy in 19th-century Germany. After a year of teaching Judaism at the Goethe University in Frankfurt/M. he returned to Israel and is now faculty member of the Department for Jewish Thought at Bar Ilan University. His book "Reading Maimonides' Philosophy" appeared in 2012, and in 2013 he published a volume on the transformation of Jewish messianism in the modern age. George lives with his wife and three children in a small village between Beer Sheva and Hebron.

Glossary / Glossar

Filip Kaźmierczak and Hanna Zoe Trauer

The glossary comprises persons, groups, and the meaning of selected technical terms. The entries are not exhaustive, rather they are meant to complement the individual contributions and support the general reader. Readers interested in learning more about a certain topic can follow up references to further readings provided at the end of most entries. The language of the entries corresponds to the language of the contributions. If a word occurs both in a German and an English contribution, it is defined in English with further readings in both languages.

Al-Andalus (Iberian Peninsula/ Iberische Halbinsel)

► Fierro ► Stroumsa ► Hasselhoff

Al-Andalus is the Arabic name for the Islamic lands in the Iberian Peninsula (today's Spain and Portugal). The Islamic rule in al-Andalus began in 711 and ended in 1492. It witnessed one of the most sophisticated developments in Arabic literature, science and philosophy. It is often mentioned as a period of great tolerance and fruitful coexistence of Islam, Judaism and Christianity, though this view has since been much criticized by scholars as an idealized picture and needs to be reviewed with more local and temporal differentiation.

Further reading

Salma Khadra Jayyusi, The Legacy of Muslim Spain, Leiden, Brill 1994.

Janina Safran, Defining Boundaries in al-Andalus. Muslims, Christians, and Jews in Islamic Iberia, Ithaca/London, Cornell University Press 2013.

Albertus Magnus

► Hasselhoff

(geb. ca. 1200 in Lauingen, gest. ca. 1280 in Köln), mittelalterlicher Universalgelehrter, Theologe und dominikanischer Bischof. Als Philosoph prägte er vor allem die christliche Aristotelesrezeption des Mittelalters. Er fertigte Paraphrasen zu fast allen aristotelischen Schriften an und befasste sich auch mit Aristoteles' Rezeption in der arabischen Philosophie. Thomas von Aquino war sein Schüler an der Pariser Universität.

Weiterführende Literatur

Walter Senner (Hg.), Albertus Magnus: zum Gedenken nach 800 Jahren. Neue Zugänge, Aspekte und Perspektiven, Berlin 2001.

Irven M. Resnick, A Companion to Albert the Great – Theology, Philosophy, and the Sciences, Leiden, Brill 2013.

Almohads

► Fierro ► Muehlethaler-M ► Stroumsa

An Islamic ► Berber dynasty that ruled over the Maghreb and ► al-Andalus from 1133 to 1269. It claimed for itself the caliphal title and the leadership of the whole Muslim community. Its name is a corruption of the Arabic *al-muwaḥḥidūn*, meaning "those who confess to the unity of God", or the Unitarians. The dynasty was based on a religious movement of this name, founded by Ibn Tūmart

(d. 1130), which concentrated on the indivisible unity of God.

Further reading
Allen J. Fromherz, The Almohads: The Rise of an Islamic Empire, London, Tauris 2010.

Almoravids
► Fierro ► Muehlethaler-M
An Islamic ► Berber dynasty that ruled in different parts of the Maghreb and ► Al-Andalus between the mid-11th and the mid-12th century AD. Its rule extended until the late 13th century in some regions of today's Tunisia and Libya. The name derives probably from the Arabic *al-murābiṭūn*, "the border warriors".

Further reading
Ronald E. Messier, The Almoravids and the Meaning of Jihad, Santa Barbara (et al.), Praeger 2010.
Heinz Halm, Die Berberreiche des Westens, in: Albert Noth/Jürgen Paul (eds.), Der islamische Orient. Grundzüge seiner Geschichte, Würzburg, Ergon-Verlag 1998, pp. 195–216.
Julia Clancy-Smith (ed.), North Africa, Islam, and the Mediterranean world: from the Almoravids to the Algerian War, London (et al.), Frank Cass 2001.

aschkenasisch
► Hasselhoff
Das europäische Judentum wird in der Geschichtsschreibung aufgrund spezifischer kultureller Entwicklungen trotz vieler lokaler Variationen grob in aschkenasische und sephardische Gemeinden eingeteilt. Als Aschkenasim werden die Juden aus nord- und osteuropäischen Ländern (Deutschland, Polen, England, Norditalien), als Sephardim die aus Südfrankreich, der ► Iberischen Halbinsel und Nordafrika bezeichnet. Die Gründe für diese Einteilung kann man in der Tatsache sehen, dass sich die Iberische Halbinsel vom 7. bis zum 15. Jh. unter muslimischer Herrschaft befand, während die späteren Aschkenasi-Gemeinden in christlichen Ländern lebten.

Ayyūbiden
► Schwarb
Eine islamische Dynastie kurdischer Abstammung, welche 1171–1249 über Ägypten, Syrien, Palästina, Jemen und Teile Mesopotamiens regierte. Sie entmachtete die ► schiitischen ► Fatimiden und setzte sich die ► sunnitische Restauration zum Ziel. Ihr Gründer und hervorragendster Vertreter war Sultan Ṣalāḥ al-Dīn al-Ayyūbī (reg. 1171–1193, in Europa unter dem Namen Saladin bekannt).

Weiterführende Literatur
R. Stephen Humphreys, From Saladin to the Mongols. The Ayyubids of Damascus, 1193–1260, Albany, State University of New York Press 1977.

al-Baghdādī, 'Abd al-Laṭīf
► Muehlethaler-T
(geb. 1162/63 in Bagdad, gest. 1231/2 ebd.) war ein islamischer Gelehrter, der von der Philosophie des Avicenna zur Philosophie von Aristoteles zurückfand. Er schrieb zu vielen Zweigen der Wissenschaft, darunter Philologie, Philosophie, Mathematik und Medizin.

Weiterführende Literatur
Cecilia Martini Bonadeo, 'Abd al-Laṭif al-Bagdadi's Philosophical Journey: from Aristotle's Metaphysics to the 'Metaphysical Science', Leiden, Brill 2013.

Berbers
► Fierro ► Muehlethaler-M
A general term for the peoples inhabiting the area west of Egypt and north of the river Niger. They speak local dialects of one language; however, there are no bi-

ological, economic or political links between all of the Berber groups. Today the term "Berber" is controversial, as it derives from the Latin, Greek and Arabic words for "Barbarian". It is often substituted by local designations or the term Amazigh.

Further reading

Michael Brett/Elizabeth Fentress, The Berbers, Oxford/Cambridge, Blackwell 1996.

Buxtorf, Johannes d. J.

► Hasselhoff

(geb. 1599 in Basel, gest. 1664 ebd.), Theologe und Orientalist. Er fertigte unter anderem lateinische Übersetzungen an, darunter 1629 eine Übersetzung des »Führers der Unschlüssigen« aus dem Hebräischen.

Weiterführende Literatur

Rudolf Smend: Vier Epitaphe – Die Basler Hebraistenfamilie Buxtorf (Litterae et Theologia 1), Berlin, de Gruyter 2010.

Crescas, Chasdai

► Muehlethaler-T

(geb. ca. 1340 in Barcelona, gest. 1410/11 in Saragossa), Philosoph und Oberhaupt der jüdischen Gemeinde von Aragon. Crescas richtete sich in seinen philosophischen Polemiken gegen das Christentum und gegen den Einfluss der aristotelischen Philosophie auf jüdische Denker. Sein Werk »Or Adonai«/»Or Haschem« versteht sich als Gegenentwurf zu Maimonides' »Führer der Unschlüssigen«; einen ► halachischen Gegenentwurf zu Maimonides' »Mišne Tora« hatte er geplant aber nicht mehr verwirklichen können.

Weiterführende Literatur

Shalom Sadik, Hasdai Crescas, in: Edward N. Zalta (ed.), The Stanford Encyclopedia of Philosophy (Spring 2014 Edition), URL = http://plato.stanford.edu/archives/spr2014/entries/crescas/.

Dhimma

► Fierro

From the Arabic word for "protection". A technical term of Islamic jurisprudence for specific religious minorities tolerated in Islamic countries. These groups were protected by the Muslim state and were neither persecuted nor forced to convert, although they were obliged to pay an additional poll-tax (*jizya*) and had limited rights in some fields like the construction of temples. The *dhimma*-groups were all monotheistic: Jews, Christians and ► Sabians. The polytheistic Hindus of India constitute an important historical exception from this rule.

Further reading

Jacob Lassner, Jews, Christians, and the Abode of Islam: Modern Scholarship, Medieval Realities. Chicago, University of Chicago Press 2012.

**al-Fārābī,
Abū Naṣr Muḥammad Ibn Muḥammad**

► Muehlethaler-M ► Muehlethaler-T

Al-Fārābī (d. 950 in Damascus) was a famous Arabic logician and philosopher in the tradition of the Neoplatonizing Aristotelism of the Alexandrian school. His approach to the philosophical and scientific curriculum became highly influential in Arabic philosophy. Maimonides considered him the foremost Logician.

Further Reading

Joep Lameer, Al-Fārābī and Aristotelian syllogistics: Greek Theory and Islamic Practice, Leiden, Brill 1994.

Fatimids (Fatimiden)

► Fierro ► Schwarb

A Shīʿite Islamic dynasty (► Shia Islam) that ruled in today's Tunisia since 909 and moved to Egypt in 973, from where it reigned until 1171. The Fatimids traced their ancestry back to the prophet Muḥammad through his daughter Fāṭima. In the eyes of the ▸ Ismāʿīlis, the Fatimid imams were the legitimate leaders of the Muslim community.

Further reading

Heinz Halm, Das Reich des Mahdi. Aufstieg der Fatimiden (875–973), München, Beck 1991.

Idem, Die Kalifen von Kairo. Die Fatimiden in Ägypten (973–1074), München, Beck 2003.

P. E. Walker, Fatimid history and Ismaili Doctrine, Aldershot, Ashgate 2008.

F. Daftary, The Ismaʿilis: Their History and Doctrines, Cambridge, Cambridge University Press 2007.

Flavius Mithridates

▸ Hasselhoff

Italienischer Gelehrter des 15. Jahrhunderts. Er fertigte zahlreiche Übersetzungen aus dem Hebräischen ins Lateinische an, unter anderem für Pico della Mirandolla.

Weiterführende Literatur

Saverio Campanini (Hg.), The Book of Bahir: Flavius Mithridates' Latin Translation, The Hebrew Text and the English Version, Torino, N. Aragno Editore 2005.

Giustiniani, Agostino

▸ Hasselhoff

(geb. 1470 in Genua, gest. 1536), Bischhof von Nebbio, Corsica, italienischer Dominikaner, Linguist und Geograph. Er lehrte u. a. an der Pariser Universität, fertigte zahlreiche Übersetzungen und Editionen an und gab 1520 in Paris Maimonides' »Führer der Unschlüssigen« auf lateinisch als »Dux seu director dubitantium aut perplexorum« heraus.

Weiterführende Literatur

Hartmut Bobzin, Agostino Giustiniani (1470–1536) und seine Bedeutung für die Geschichte der Arabistik, in Zeitschrift der Deutschen Morgenländischen Gesellschaft, Supplement 8 (1990), 131–139.

Genizah (Genisa)

▸ Muehlethaler-M ▸ Schwarb

is the name for a storage space, usually in a synagogue, that is used to conceal disused texts which cannot be destroyed due to halakhic precepts. The Genizah of the Ibn Ezra synagogue in Fusṭāṭ-Miṣr (Old Cairo) was in constant use for several hundred years. In the 19th century, scholars moved many of the documents it contained, the oldest of which date from the 10th century, to Europe. They can be found in collections of several libraries in the West, most notably in the library of Cambridge University.

Further Reading

Stefan C. Reif, A Jewish Archive from Old Cairo. The History of Cambridge University's Genizah Collection, Richmond, Curzon 2000.

Adina Hoffman/Peter Cole, Sacred Trash: The Lost and Found World of the Cairo Geniza, New York, Nextbook, Schocken 2010.

halachisch

▸ Hasselhoff

(hebr. »halach«: gehen); Halacha bezeichnet den jüdischen Lebenswandel betreffende Anleitungen und Vorschriften. Die bekanntesten halachischen Werke des rabbinischen Judentums sind ▸ Mischna und ▸ Talmud, welche bis in die Neuzeit hinein immer neue Kommentare und Kodifikationen nach sich zogen. Unter den Werken Maimonides' befinden sich zwei wesentlich halachische Werke, sein Mischna-Kommentar (»Kitāb al-Sirāj«)

und die als Kompilation der gesamten Halacha angelegte »Mišne Tora«. Außerdem schrieb Maimonides Gutachten zu halachischen Fragen.

al-Harizi, Yehuda

► Hasselhoff

(Yaḥyā b. Sulaymān al-Ḥarīzī, geb. ca. 1165 in Aleppo, gest. 1225 ebd.), war Poet und Übersetzer vom Arabischen ins Hebräische. Er fertigte unter anderem eine hebräische Übersetzung von Maimonides' Mischna-Kommentar und den »Führer der Unschlüssigen« an. (Zum Verhältnis seiner Übersetzung zur Übersetzung Samuel ibn Tibbons ► Tibboniden.)

Weiterführende Literatur

Victor Emanuel Reichelt (Übers.), The Tahkemoni of Judah al-Harizi: An English Translation, Jerusalem, R. H. Cohen's Press 1965.

J. Sedan, Yehūda al-Ḥarīzī en tant que carrefour culturel: une biographie arabe d'un auteur juif, Göttingen 1997.

Haskalah (Maskilim)

► Melamed ► Kohler

(Hebr. education), so-called Jewish Enlightenment that began in Germany in the late 18th century. Moses Mendelssohn (1729–1786) is considered the founder of the Haskalah movement.

Further reading

Michael A. Meyer, The Origins of the Modern Jew, Detroit, Wayne State University Press 1976.

Ibn al-ʿArabī, Muḥyī al-Dīn

► Fierro

(b. 1165 in Murcia, d. 1240 in Damascus) Also known under the name *al-Shaykh al-Akbar*, "the greatest master", he was a mystic (► Sufism) and an Islamic scholar from ► al-Andalus who spent most of his life in Eastern lands. His works include more than 200 volumes concerned with all fields including Islamic jurisprudence, theology and philosophy. The theory of the "unity of being" (*waḥdat al-wujūd*) is considered to have originated in his books. He himself, however, never used this term.

Further reading

Toshihiko Izutsu, A Comparative Study of the Key Philosophical Concepts in Taoism and Sufism, Tokyo, 1966 (second edition: Sufism and Taoism, Los Angeles, University of California Press 1983).

Michel Chodkiewicz, An Ocean without Shore: Ibn ʿArabî, the Book, and the Law, translated from the French by David Streight, Albany, NY, State University of New York Press 1993.

Ronald J. Nettler, Sufi Metaphysics and Quranic Prophets: Ibn ʿArabi's Thought and Method in the Fusus al-Hikam, Oxford, Islamic Texts Society 2003.

Ibn al-ʿAssāl, Al-Asʿad Abū al-Farāj Hibatullāh

► Schwarb

Koptischer Intellektueller und einer der Awlād al-ʿAssāl (»der Söhne von Faḫr ad-Daula Abū l-Mufaḍḍal Asʿad al-ʿAssāl«), einer Gruppe von vier (Halb-)Brüdern welche im 13. Jhd. zur koptischen Kulturblüte durch ihre Schriften über die Grammatik sowie die Theologie, Philosophie und christliche Bibelexegese beigetragen haben. Sie waren in der ► ayyūbidischen Administration angestellt und beherrschten neben dem Arabischen auch Griechisch, Koptisch und Syro-Aramäisch. Ihre besondere Aktivität fällt ungefähr auf die Zeit zwischen 1230 und 1270.

Weiterführende Literatur

Georg Graf, Die koptische Gelehrtenfamilie der Aulâd al-ʿAssâl und ihr Schrifttum, in: Orientalia, Neue Serie Band 1, 1932, S. 34–56, 129–148, 193–204

Ibn Bājja, Abū Bakr Muḥammad Ibn Yaḥyā
► Muehlethaler-T
(latinisiert als Avempace; geb. 1085 in Al-Andalus, gest. um 1139), einer der ersten muslimischen Philosophen in al-Andalus. Besonders seine Kommentare zu Werken Aristoteles' und seine Überlegungen zum intellektuellen Nachleben des Menschen wurden rezipiert.

Weiterführende Literatur
Alexander Altmann, Ibn Bâjja on Man's Ultimate Felicity, in: Harry Austryn Wolfson Jubilee Volume, English Section, Jerusalem, American Academy for Jewish Research, Band 1, 1965, 65–70.
Charles Genequand, La conduite de l'isolé et deux autres épîtres (Epître de l'adieu; Conjonction de l'intellect). Introduction, édition critique du texte arabe, traduction et commentaire, Paris, Vrin 2010.

Ibn Rushd, Abū al-Walīd Muḥammad Ibn Aḥmad (Averroes)
► Fierro ► Muehlethaler-T
(b. 1126 in Cordoba, d. 1198 in Marrakesh), was an Islamic scholar, jurisprudent, theologian and philosopher (an Aristotelian). He also acted as judge for the ► Almohads. He acquired fame primarily through his numerous commentaries on almost every work of Aristotle. These works earned him the sobriquet "The Commentator".

Further reading
Oliver Leaman, Averroes and his Philosophy, Oxford, Clarendon Press 1988.
Dominique Urvoy, Ibn Rushd (Averroes), transl. by O. Stewart, London/New York, Routledge 1991.

Ibn Sīnā, Abū 'Alī al-Ḥusayn Ibn 'Abd Allāh (Avicenna)
► Muehlethaler-T
(geb. 980 bei Buchara, gest. 1037 in Hamadan). Avicenna ist eine zentrale Figur der arabischen Philosophie, Medizin und Wissenschaft aus dem Osten der islamischen Welt. Seine philosophischen und medizinischen Werke entfalteten aber auch im lateinischen Europa eine große und nachhaltige Wirkung.

Weiterführende Literatur
Jon McGinnis, Avicenna, Oxford, Oxford University Press 2010.
Dimitri Gutas, Avicenna and the Aristotelian Tradition, Leiden, Brill 2014.

Ibn Ṭufayl, Abū Bakr Muḥammad
► Fierro
A physician and philosopher from ► al-Andalus (b. ca. 1105, d. 1185/86). He served as court physician for the ► Almohad caliphs, managed some cities, among others Cordoba, and brought the young ► Averroes to the attention of the Almohad caliph. His best-known book, *Ḥayy ibn Yaqẓān* ("The Living, Son of the Waking One", trans. into Latin as "Philosophus autodidactus") is a philosophical novel stating that philosophy is the best tool for understanding God. In Latin he is known as Abubacer.

Further reading
Ibn Tufayl/Lenn Evan Goodman (Ed.), Ibn Tufayl's Hayy Ibn Yaqzān: A Philosophical Tale, New York, Twayne 1972.
Patric O. Schaerer, Abū Bakr ibn Ṭufail. Der Philosoph als Autodidakt: Ḥayy ibn Yaqẓān. Ein philosophischer Insel-Roman, Hamburg, Meiner Verlag 2004.

Islamic legal schools
► Fierro
Each school of legal thought in Islam (*madhhab*, pl. *madhāhib*) follows its own clas-

sification of the sources of law, the most important of the latter being: the Koran, prophetic traditions (*ḥadīth*), consensus of the believers (*ijmāʿ*) and analogy (*qiyās*). The four so-called canonic *madhāhib* of ▸ Sunni Islam that recognize each other as legitimate are: Mālikiyya, Ḥanafiyya, Ḥanbaliyya and Shāfiʿiyya. In addition, there are numerous smaller schools, like the Ẓāhiriyya, which are not important nowadays in terms of numbers.

Further reading

Wael B. Hallaq, A History of Islamic Legal Theories. An Introduction to Sunnī uṣūl al-fiqh, Cambridge, Cambridge University Press 1999.

Ismaʿiliyya (Ismāʿīliyya)

▸ Fierro

A group of ▸ Shia Islam, Ismāʿīlites share with other Shiites the belief in supernatural capacities of the Imams (the descendants of the Prophet through his son-in-law and nephew ʿAlī). They are also known as 'Seveners'. The Ismāʿīliyya became first known as a revolutionary underground organisation in Iraq and Persia in the 9th century and spread from there into the whole Islamic world, with lasting presence in Yemen, North Africa, northern parts of the Indian subcontinent and Syria.

Further reading

Farhad Daftary, The Ismāʿīlis. Their History and Doctrines, Cambridge, Cambridge University Press 1990.

Johannes von Capua

▸ Hasselhoff

(geb. ca. 1250 in Capua, gest. ca. 1310 in Rom), italienischer, jüdischer Autor und Übersetzer, zum Christentum konvertiert. Er übersetzte mehrere Werke aus der arabischen Sprache ins Lateinische, darunter Teile aus Maimonides' medizinischem Werk.

Weiterführende Literatur

Görge K. Hasselhoff, Johannes von Capua und Armengaud Blaise als Übersetzer medizinischer Werke des Maimonides, in: Andreas Speer/Lydia Wegener (Hg.), Wissen über Grenzen. Arabisches Wissen und lateinisches Mittelalter, Berlin/New York 2006.

Judaeo-Arabic

▸ Stroumsa

A middle-Arabic dialect used by Jews in Arab lands. It was often written in Hebrew letters and incorportated Hebrew words and quotations. Judaeo-Arabic was distinct from the literary language of the Muslim elite, which orientated itself to classical Arabic, the language of the Koran.

Kopten

▸ Schwarb

Ein Allgemeinbegriff für die Einwohner Ägyptens vor der islamischen Eroberung 641 und Anhänger des koptischen Christentums. Die koptische Sprache war die letzte Entwicklung des Ägyptischen und wurde in der koptischen Schrift geschrieben, welche das griechische Alphabet mit einigen demotischen Buchstaben verbindet. Die ägyptischen Kopten waren Monophysiten, d. h. sie glaubten, Christus habe in einer Natur seine Menschlichkeit und Göttlichkeit vereint. Wegen dieser Überzeugung wurden sie nach dem Konzil von Kalchedon (451), auf welchem der Monophysitismus verurteilt wurde, verstärkt verfolgt. Die arabisch-islamische Eroberung wurde von ihnen in dieser Hinsicht positiv aufgenommen. Die Kopten erhielten unter der islamischen Vorherrschaft den Status einer ▸ *dhimma*-Gemeinschaft und führten die Administration des Staates. Außer während einiger kurzer Episoden wurden sie nicht verfolgt und genossen vielmehr eine privilegierte soziale Stellung. Für eine lange Zeit bildeten sie noch die Mehrheit der Gesellschaft, und ihre Arabisierung und Islamisierung schritt nur langsam voran. Erst unter den Mamluken (1250–1517) verschlechterte sich ihre Lage, obwohl sie immer noch die administrative Elite des Staates bildeten.

Weiterführende Literatur

Kamal Sabri Kolta, Christentum im Land der Pharaonen: Geschichte und Gegenwart der Kopten in Ägypten, München, 1985.

Kurt J. Werthmuller, Coptic Identity and Ayyubid Politics in Egypt 1218–1250, Cairo, American University of Cairo Press 2010.

Madrasa

▸ Fierro

Arabic for "school", *madrasa* was a school and living complex with a mosque. This type of educational institution blossomed and spread in the Islamic world in the 11th century.

Further reading

Nicole Grandin, Madrasa: la transmission du savoir dans le monde musulman, Paris, Éditions Arguments 1997.

Mahdī

▸ Fierro

Arabic for "the rightly-guided one", *mahdī* describes in numerous Islamic traditions the person who will come at the end of times to unite the whole world under his rule and bring it peace and justice. Since this belief spread among Muslim communities, many rulers and religious leaders claimed this title. This is especially true for Shiites (like the ▸ Ismāʿīlite ▸ Fatimids), mystical leaders and religious revolutionaries (like the first ▸ Almohad preacher Ibn Tūmart), who sought to emphasize through this term their turning away from traditions and towards new forms of religiosity.

Further reading

David Cook, Studies in Muslim Apocalyptic, Princeton, Darwin Press 2002.

Meister Eckhart

▸ Hasselhoff

Eckhart von Hochheim (geb. ca. 1260 in Hochheim, gest. 1327/1328 in Avignon) war ein mittelalterlicher Philosoph und Theologe, Dominikaner. 1326 wurde gegen ihn ein Verfahren wegen Häresie eröffnet, er starb jedoch vor dessen Beendigung in Avignon.

Weiterführende Literatur

Norbert Winkler, Meister Eckhart zur Einführung, in: Mojsisch, Burkhard/Olaf Pluta/Rudolf Rehn (Hg.), Bochumer Philosophisches Jahrbuch für Antike und Mittelalter, Band 4, Bochum 1999.

Midrash

▸ Muehlethaler-M ▸ Stroumsa

Midrash (hebr. "darash": to search) refers to the interpretation of the Bible, mostly in the ▸ Rabbinic era. There are ▸ halakhic midrashim that deal with the interpretation of legal texts and haggadic midrashim that interpret non-legal parts of the Bible, often adding further narratives about biblical personalities.

Mishnah (Mischna)

▸ Kohler ▸ Muehlethaler-M ▸ Schwarb

The Mishnah (ca. 200 CE) is the first compilation of the ▸ Halakha. It entailed a long literary tradition, including the Palestinian and Babylonian ▸ Talmud, whose production was initiated immediately after its completion. The tradition of commentaries continued until modern times. Maimonides also wrote a commentary on the Mishnah (*Kitāb al-Sirāj*).

Münster, Sebastian
► Hasselhoff
(geb. 1488 in Nieder-Ingelheim, gest. 1552 in Basel), deutscher Hebraist, Humanist und Kosmograph. Unter anderem veröffentlichte er eine Fassung der hebräischen Bibel mit lateinischer Übersetzung.

Weiterführende Literatur
Karl Heinz Burmeister, Sebastian Münster – Versuch eines biographischen Gesamtbildes, Basel [u. a.] 1963.

Nestorian Christians
► Stroumsa
A Christian community claiming the distinction between the human and godly natures of Jesus. Its eponym, Nestorius, was Bishop of Constantinople (428–431) and was anathematized at the Council of Ephesus. The Council of Chalcedon (451) confirmed the condemnation of the Nestorian creed. Because of the Byzantine persecution many members of the group fled to the East, and their descendants are now gathered in the Assyrian Church of the East.

Nicolaus Cusanus
► Hasselhoff
(geb. 1401 an der Mosel, gest. 1464 in Umbrien), deutscher Philosoph, Theologe und Kardinal. In seinen neuplatonisch geprägten Schriften finden sich zahlreiche Bezüge zu mittelalterlichen und antiken Philosophen. Dionysius der Kartäuser (geb. ca. 1402/3, gest. 1471), niederländischer Philosoph und Theologe, begleitete Nicolaus Cusanus auf seiner Visitationsreise durch die Niederlande.

Weiterführende Literatur
Norbert Winkler, Nikolaus von Kues zur Einführung, Hamburg, Junius, 2001.
Emery Kent, Einführung in Dionysii Cartvsiensis Opera selecta, Tvrnholti, Brepols 1991.

Ostjudentum
► Kohler
(lit: "Eastern Jewry") is a general term used mainly by German Jews in the 19th and 20th century to refer to the (immigrant) Jews from Eastern Europe. The term implied mostly the more traditional, less assimilated and often Yiddish-speaking Jews.

Qibla
► Fierro
denotes the direction towards which Muslims pray, which is the *Ka'ba* in Mecca. All mosques have a *miḥrāb*, or a prayer niche, showing exactly this direction. The orientation of the mosques has always required a profound knowledge of mathematics and astronomy. The *qibla* is also important for other reasons than prayer, e. g., animals to be slaughtered are held with their heads in that direction, and the dead are to be buried facing it.

Rabbi Dov Ber of Mezerich
► Melamed
The "Maggid" (= preacher) of Mezerich, was the successor of Israel ben Eliezer (the "Baal Shem Tov") in the role of the leader of the 18th century Eastern European Hasidic movement, which combined traditional Judaism with kabbalistic tendencies.

Rabbinic (Rabbinisch)
► Hasselhoff ► Kohler ► Melamed
► Muehlethaler-M ► Schwarb
The Rabbinic era began after the destruction of the Second Temple by the Romans (70 CE). Rabbinic Judaism is considered to have emerged from the Pharisaic school, one of the Jewish schools of thought during the Second Temple period. Well-known works of Rabbinic literature are, among others, the ► Mishnah and the ► Talmud.

Reformjudentum
► Kohler
Reformjudentum refers to the Reform movement in Judaism in 19th-century Germany under the influence of ► Haskalah and assimilation. The reformers wanted to give Judaism a modern and philosophically more consistent theology. In practice, they especially sought to revive the synagogal ritual, e.g., by using German in prayer books and services, the introduction of the organ into the service and the abolition of the separation of men and women during the service.

Further reading
Michael A Meyer, Response to Modernity: A History of the Reform Movement in Judaism, New York, Wayne State University Press 1988.

Rosenzweig, Franz
► Kohler
(b. 1886 in Kassel, d. 1929 in Frankfurt/Main), Jewish historian and philosopher; Rosenzweig studied under Hermann Cohen at the »Hochschule für die Wissenschaft des Judentums« (Higher Institute for Jewish Studies) in Berlin.

Sabians (Sabäer)
► Schwarb ► Stroumsa
A name for at least two religious groups. The first group is mentioned in the Koran as a religion of the book (*ahl al-kitāb*; II 62; V 69; XXII 17). From the beginning of Koranic exegesis it has been unclear which community is actually meant by this term. We know only that it was a monotheistic religion. The second group is supposed to have lived in what is today Southwest Turkey and professed a polytheistic Semitic religion. These people were the subject of *The Nabatean Agriculture*, a book used by Maimonides and assumed to have been written by Ibn Waḥshiyya.

Sasanians
► Stroumsa
An Iranian dynasty that ruled from the 3rd to 7th century C. E. Its empire stretched from the Indus to the Tigris and Euphrates, and included parts of Arabia and modern Georgia, extending at its peak to the Levante and Egypt. The state religion of the Sasanian state was ► Zoroastrianism. One of the greatest empires of its time, it fought against Rome and then Byzantium. Its cultural influence was felt as far as Europe and China, and it shaped the Islamic culture after the Arab conquest occurred in 651.

Shia Islam
► Fierro ► Stroumsa
One of the two main Islamic communities that developed as a result of a religious and political conflict (► Sunni Islam). Its name originates from the phrase "shīʿat ʿAlī" ("the party of ʿAlī"), which stems from the Shiites' belief that ʿAlī (r. 656–661), the nephew and son-in-law of the prophet Muḥammad, was Muḥammad's designated heir and therefore the legitimate caliph. Consequently, they believe that the right to the caliphate remained in the house of ʿAlī. The first leaders of Shia, the imams, are believed to have had special contact with God, and some of their statements, the so-called "traditions of the imams", are considered to be important sources of religious law, which distinguishes Shia from Sunni jurisprudence.

Further reading
Heinz Halm, Die Schiiten, München 2005.
Mavani, Hamid. Religious authority and political thought in Twelver Shi'ism: from Ali to post-Khomeini. London [et al.], Routledge 2013.
Husain Naṣr (ed.). Shiʿism: Doctrines, thought, and spirituality. Albany, State University of New York Press 1988.

Sufism

► Fierro

A term including diverse Islamic groups (Arabic *ṭarīqa*—“path”) that believe in direct contact with God through mystical experience. Their communal prayers (Arab. *dhikr*) are often accompanied by music and dancing, sometimes ecstatic. Sufi groups have sometimes been persecuted by radical scholars because of their spiritual interpretation of the religious sources.

Further reading

Alexander Knysh, Islamic Mysticism. A Short History, Leiden, Brill 2000.

Sunni Islam

► Fierro ► Stroumsa

One of the two main Islamic communities that developed as a result of a religious and political conflict (► Shia Islam). Sunnites rejected ʿAlīs exclusive claim for the leadership of the Muslim community. As a way of distinguishing themselves from the Shia they called themselves *ahl al-sunna wa-l-jamāʿa*, “people of the tradition and community”, i.e., those who follow the example of the prophet Muḥammad and stick to the Muslim community, or those who do not separate themselves from it.

Further reading

Jonathan Porter Berkey, The Formation of Islam: Religion and Society in the Near East, 600–1800, Cambridge, Cambridge University Press 2003.

Gerhard Endreß, Der Islam. Einführung in seine Geschichte, München 1997.

Talmud (Babylonian/Babylonischer Talmud)

► Hasselhoff ► Kohler ► Muehlethaler-M

The Babylonian Talmud (compiled between the 3rd and 8th century CE) is one of the most significant texts of ► Rabbinic Judaism and is considered canonical in contemporary Judaism. The term “Talmud” usually refers to the ► Mishnah and the Gemara, which consists of ► halakhic and aggadic discussions and commentaries to the mishnaic text. From the Middle Ages on, many Christian attacks against Judaism focused on the Talmud, often leading to (forced) disputations, Jews having to defend the Talmud, and even burnings of copies of the Talmud. The first of such burnings took place in Paris in 1242 following a public disputation in 1240. It was caused by Nicholas Donin, a Jew who had converted to Christianity in 1236 and had written a composition of charges against the Talmud.

Thomas von Aquino

► Hasselhoff

(geb. ca. 1225 bei Aquino, gest. 1274 in Fossanova), mittelalterlicher Philosoph und Theologe, Dominikaner. Er war an der Pariser Universität Sorbonne ein Schüler des Albertus Magnus, von dessen Aristotelesrezeption er stark beeinflusst wurde. Wie dieser verfasste er zahlreiche Kommentare zu aristotelischen Schriften.

Weiterführende Literatur

Rolf Schönberger, Thomas von Aquin zur Einführung, 4. Aufl., Hamburg 2012.

Leo Elders, The Philosophical Theology of St. Thomas Aquinas, Leiden, Brill 1990.

Tibboniden, Samuel ibn Tibbon

► Hasselhoff ► Muehlethaler-T

Die Tibboniden sind eine jüdische Übersetzerfamilie des 12. und 13. Jahrhunderts, auf deren Mitglieder zahlreiche Übersetzungen, v. a. philosophischer Werke aus dem Arabischen ins Hebräische, zurückgehen. Samuel bin Tibbon (1160–1230) fertigte die erste vollständige hebräische Übersetzung des »Dalālat alḥāʾirīn« als

»More Nevuḫim« in Zusammenarbeit mit Maimonides an, die Grundlage für zahlreiche spätere Übertragungen wurde.

Weiterführende Literatur

James T. Robinson, Samuel Ibn Tibbon, in: The Stanford Encyclopedia of Philosophy (Spring 2014 Edition), Edward N. Zalta (ed.), URL = http://plato.stanford.edu/archives/spr2014/entries/tibbon/.

Wellhausen, Julius

► Kohler

(geb. 1844 in Hameln, gest. 1918 in Göttingen), German historian, theologian and orientalist, famous mainly for his historical research on the Hebrew Bible. He was occasionally reproached for anti-Semitic tendencies in his work.

Further reading

Rudolf Smend, Julius Wellhausen. Ein Bahnbrecher in drei Disziplinen, München 2006.

Wilhelm von Auvergne

► Hasselhoff

(geb. ca. 1180 in Aurillac, gest. 1249 in Paris), französischer Bischof, Theologe und Philosoph, befasste sich als einer der ersten unter den christlichen Philosophen mit der jüdischen und islamischen Aristotelesrezeption.

Weiterführende Literatur

Jan Rohls, Wilhelm von Auvergne und der mittelalterliche Aristotelismus. Gottesbegriff und aristotelischer Philosophie zwischen Augustin und Thomas von Aquin, München 1980.

Windelband, Wilhelm, and Rickert, Heinrich

► Kohler

Windelband (b. 1848 in Potsdam, d. 1915 in Heidelberg) and Rickert (b. 1863 in Danzig, d. 1936 in Heidelberg) were German philosophers and exponents of the so-called "Southwest School" or "Baden School" of Neo-Kantianism. This school stands in contrast to the so-called Marburg school, of which Hermann Cohen was the main representative.

Further reading

Frederick C. Beiser, The German Historicist Tradition, Oxford, Oxford University Press 2011.

Wissenschaft des Judentums

► Kohler

("scientific study of Judaism") is a term for the early research of Jewish history and literature from the early 19th century on, e.g., by Leopold Zunz, Abraham Geiger and Heinrich Graetz. Centres of this research became the "Breslau Rabbinical Seminary" (*Jüdisch-Theologisches Seminar in Breslau*), the first institution for the training of rabbis in Germany, founded in 1854, and the "College for the Scientific Study of Judaism" (*Hochschule für die Wissenschaft des Judentums*) in Berlin, founded in 1872, where Herman Cohen taught in his latter days.

Further Reading

Andreas Gotzmann et al. (eds.), Modern Judaism and Historical, Consciousness: Identities, Encounters, Perspectives, Leiden, Brill 2007.

Wolffians

► Melamed

Named after Christian Wolff (b. 1679 in Breslau, d. 1754 in Halle), a German philosopher of the Enlightenment, whose adherents (Wolffians) had great influence in 18th-century Germany. Moses Mendelssohn is also considered to be a Wolffian.

Zohar

► Melamed

The Zohar (hebr. "Splendor") is the main work of Kabbalah. It was ascribed to Rabbi

Simeon bar Yochai (2nd century). The real author was probably Moshe ben Shem-Tov de León, who compiled it in the 13th century in Spain.

Further reading

Arthur Green, A guide to the Zohar, Stanford, Stanford University Press 2004.

Zoroastrianism (Anhänger Zoroasters)
▸ Schwarb ▸ Stroumsa

A religion that developed in the 6th century B.C.E. and was named after an Iranian prophet Zoroaster (also: Zarathustra). It combined dualistic and monotheistic ideas and influenced in various ways the three monotheistic religions.